The Bundle

First produced by the Royal Shakespeare Company at the Warehouse in January 1978, *The Bundle* returns to the subject of one of Bond's earlier plays – *Narrow Road to the Deep North* (1968). Both plays take as their starting point an incident in the life of the seventeenth century Japanese poet, Basho, who rejects the chance to save a child's life and instead sets out on a solitary journey in search of enlightenment. But from this same opening the story of *The Bundle* unfolds very differently: the child survives, not, as in the first play, to be a tyrant, but to liberate the oppressed, achieving his aims with the help of a gang of former bandits and himself confronting the dilemma Basho confronted in pursuit of his goal. Of the play the author himself has said: 'One of the things I've tried to do in *The Bundle* is to demystify the use of moral argument so that we can't be morally blackmailed any more. In order to change society structurally, you may find yourself doing what is, in quotes, wrong.'

'. . . a complex and marvellously written play'.

Irving Wardle, *The Times*

'. . . it has the force and the onward movement of a tidal wave. It communicates narrative joy; a complicated tale is to be told, spanning many years, and the playwright's craft in keeping us aware of our bearings is immaculate.'

Robert Cushman, *Observer*

The volume also contains an introduction by the author and *The Bundle Poems* written at the same time as the play.

The photograph on the front of the cover shows Mike Gwilym, Meg Davies and Paul Moriarty in the Royal Shakespeare Company production of The Bundle *at the Warehouse Theatre, London. Both this and the photograph of Edward Bond on the back of the cover is reproduced by courtesy of Chris Davies.*

Edward Bond

THE BUNDLE

or

New Narrow Road to the Deep North

EYRE METHUEN

LONDON

First published 1978 by Eyre Methuen Ltd
11 New Fetter Lane, London EC4P 4EE
© *1978 by Edward Bond*
Printed in Great Britain by
Cox & Wyman Ltd, Fakenham, Norfolk

ISBN 0 413 39350 x (*Hardback*)
ISBN 0 413 39360 7 (*Paperback*)

For Sue and Howard Davies

A Note on Dramatic Method

Human consciousness is not an innate quality that creates itself. We have an innate capacity for consciousness. How we become conscious is largely decided by our society and its institutions – the family, schools, courts, media and so forth – and by the organization and practice of our work, the means by which we live. Human consciousness is a creation of society and takes historical forms. The nature of human consciousness at any time is a consequence of the particular society in which it is created.

Societies change and human consciousness changes with them. Change originates from technology, which constantly changes the way in which people work, in which they sustain their life. This provokes changes in human consciousness and subsequently in social institutions. Changes in human consciousness begin before changes in social institutions because, although working people have the first experience of using new technology (in this connection working people must be thought of as workers and consumers), they are not usually in control of social institutions. And furthermore, social institutions usually resist change. There are at least two reasons for this. Firstly, in order to function efficiently society must observe certain instrumental values. Cars must normally be driven on one side of the road, promises kept, rules of hygiene respected and so forth. These rules or regulations are not in themselves moral values. You can keep a promise to kill an innocent person, or swerve across the road to miss a pedestrian. But it is morally valuable that they should normally be kept. Without them society is not possible. Secondly, social institutions represent the interest of the ruling class. They developed when technology was simpler than it is now and they represent a social order – a relationship between social institutions, technology, environment and human consciousness – which technology has made obsolescent. Our social institutions do not represent the

interests of those people who by experience as workers and consumers are creating developments in human consciousness, new ways of understanding and interpreting the world, and so making necessary new ways of organizing it. But when the ruling class defends its interests it can claim it acts for the good of everyone because it controls the administration, the mechanical efficiency, of society (keeping to the right side of the road and so forth) – and this claim has an obvious plausibility.

Social institutions control law, education, civic force (police and armed forces), scientific research and so on – all the machinery and knowledge we need to live together and create a common life. But the control is deeper. It permeates the ordinary use of language, mores, customs, common assumptions and unquestioned ideas. Together these things – institutions and their social reflections – make up a tacitly accepted view of life, a consciousness of the world which is also in large part a self-consciousness. It is not the whole of self-consciousness because, as I've said, that is partly created by experience as worker and consumer. This experience brings the tacitly accepted, ruling-class, institutional values into confrontation with moral values. Moral values originate in the relationship between men, their technology, their environment and their mutual interdependence. They are not, therefore, necessarily embodied in the structure of any particular society. We can talk of a tacitly accepted view of the world because although this view is often rejected – in industrial strikes for example – it remains powerful unless experience as worker and consumer is transposed into concepts, and then into customs, mores and so forth to make up a radically changed view of the world. Social institutions control the tacitly accepted view by means of education, the selection of information, economic sanctions and if necessary naked force. Above all they control the tacitly accepted *moral* code – and social living requires a moral code (or a reactionary substitute for it) as well as a set of rules. But social institutions do not create culture. Ultimately culture derives from our experience as workers and consumers; and a

culture is created by working people bringing social institutions, economic and political organization, into line with their experience and needs as workers and consumers. When that isn't done society is not an agent of law and order but of regulation and force; it is not a guardian of morality, it merely administers (or rather struggles necessarily unsuccessfully to administer) mechanical efficiency. For a society to administer moral law, its institutions, and their reflection in mores, language, expectations etc., must work in harmony with the new self-consciousness developed by working people as workers and consumers. Society requires its members to have certain attitudes to its institutions, to understand the justification for them, to respect and consent to them. Otherwise, instead of relying on understanding, the institutions must rely on lies, force or reaction. Yet a changing technology creates new attitudes and knowledge in those who use it and benefit from it: self-autonomy in place of servitude, a technical interpretation of the world in place of a mythological one, a new image of the self. These attitudes cannot work efficiently, harmoniously, with obsolescent institutions. When technology, social institutions and human consciousness reflect each other's exigencies and possibilities in a rational way, then there is harmony in the organization of life, difficulties are solved rationally, and society can be said to administer moral law. The effort to create such a society, to derive concepts from experience and to develop mores and habits that go beyond immediate, opportunistic, individual interests, is the practical work of creating culture – and this itself brings further changes in human consciousness. Culture is not a static condition administered by social institutions that are its permanent repositories. Culture is provoked by technological change and achieved through the need human beings have to harmonize their experience of sustaining their life with their experience of society, so that a new form of self-consciousness is created.

When a new human self-consciousness, adequate to living in the present and preparing the future, is not being created, human self-consciousness becomes reactionary. Then there are calls for a

return to the past in attitudes and organization, and in the imagery (uniforms, architecture, art and so forth) which give social institutions prestige and authority. In the ruling class this is a desire to return to the mode of the eighteenth-century gentleman of enlightenment or to some even more remote historical-mythological birth of the nation. For the working class it means Disneyland or Cloud Cuckoo Land. Then human beings become increasingly barbaric and aggressive. This is partly because they have emotional attitudes to what they think and partly because the organization of their lives has physiological consequences. In conditions of tension people are more readily aggressive and credulous. Usually we assume that when people are destructive that is because they are motivated by unconscious emotional attitudes which make them behave atavistically. But I think they behave like this because of the conditions society allocates to them and because of the tensions of holding an absurd society together. A society which tries to create a self-consciousness based on imagery, organization and attitudes from the past will cause emotional crises in its members that must result in violence and aggression. They either struggle to resist, as any prisoner might, or become dangerously apathetic so that they do not protest at the inhumanities of their reactionary regime, or even become its brutal accomplices. That is the sum total of the forces of human darkness, the original sin or natural aggression, which the ruling class seizes on so avidly and teaches so assiduously.

Self-consciousness is created in the process of understanding the world and our own behaviour. It is necessary to create a new human self-consciousness for our own time, our technology, our society, ourselves. This self-consciousness must be based on a consciousness of the world and an interpretation of it. One can say that socialist consciousness is equivalent to moral self-consciousness in that it is a viable knowledge of the self in relation to practical involvement in the world; this self-consciousness contains not merely experience but unites it with an interpretation of the world and self that restores moral action to our lives. Per-

haps one should not even use the concept 'self' in connection with reaction because the reactionary self is only a neurotic or opportunistic parasite on the past: it is ghost-like. A valid self-consciousness is not this ghost-like, wraith-like experience; it has the feel of the world. It is not sufficient for someone to be told that someone else is good or bad and to understand this in terms of reward or punishment. Morality cannot be conditioned because it involves free choice. The practical realities of goodness and badness must be apparent, discernible. If an apple is to be eaten it must look, smell, taste, feel and (when tapped) sound good. And we must know, through our conceptual understanding of the world, that eating it will not destroy moral social relationships (in the metaphysics of christianity, that it is not interdicted by god: the original crime was not murder but theft of the master's property – Cain slew Abel *after* the apple was stolen). Human consciousness, to be practical, requires a wholeness of understanding that has many similarities to this. Conceptual ideas alone cannot create this wholeness. The elements of a man's understanding must relate to one another so that he has a sound, reliable interpretation of the world not merely in terms of concept but also in justified expectation. His experience must be the ground for sound judgement and hope. In this way he can live without absurdity or too much tension and can interpret himself in terms of the world and his society.

Art is one way of creating this wholeness of understanding, and theatre is one of the arts best suited to do this. Theatre can validate human standards, ways of living, ethical decisions, understanding, by demonstrating the relation of cause and effect in practical human life and not merely in concept or theory. This is ultimately a demonstration of the soundness or unsoundness of these standards, methods, interpretations and decisions. In this way experience is not merely recorded randomly but is set in a moral order of reason and judgement. An audience can then see what human beings are and what are the standards, practices and

concepts by which they should live. In this way human consciousness is changed.

Art is sometimes said to be a reflection of the ideal. This could mean it is not a guide to action. Yet when in a sense art makes the ideal concrete for the present it must also be a guide to present action. It is not a narcotic or dream. Art portrays present-day human beings who are conscious, or potentially conscious, of a utopian society – and who desire to achieve it. It shows the desire, the possibility, the action necessary to achieve it, and the practical standards that can be used to assess this action and the moral standards that can be used to judge it. These standards are one assurance that the possibility is real. Art doesn't create a void between our world and a rational world. Sometimes the act of trying to achieve this future may cause immediate unhappiness, but this is certainly the only form of cultural action possible in our time. That is why socialist art is not superficial or merely programmatic, but includes the whole of human experience, tragic and comic. And in our time only socialism can produce art because it unites experience of the world and society with the rational understanding of them and with an optimistic interpretation of our present condition. It interprets the world, it does not merely mirror it. The alternative is the despair or dreary cynicism of the theatre of the absurd, which still passes for culture in our schools and universities.

Why is theatre so well suited to help to create self-consciousness? It does not use aspects of human beings in the way painting and novels do, but puts human beings themselves on stage. Audiences judge not merely by what actors say but by how they say it, how they move, how and where they look, gesture, interact. Human acts are then not judged by their theoretical correctness, nor oddly enough by their putative inevitability, but by their concrete plausibility to the audience, who are after all actors in their own lives. The stage does not go inside the mind as easily as novels and music can, but it can demonstrate social relationships between people more concretely than other arts. All theatre is political –

Coward's as well as Brecht's – and theatre always emphasizes the social in art. The audience judges in the same complex way that it judges in ordinary life. But it is given this advantage: it may look at things it would normally run from in fear, turn from in embarrassment, prevent in anger, or pass by because they are hidden, either purposefully or innocently. So audiences respond with all the faculties of their consciousness to the things that determine their social and private lives. They judge and in judging extend their self-consciousness because they have not merely responded to a situation or character in the socially prescribed way (as conditioned by institutions and tacitly accepted mores) but have been made to see aspects of the situation or character which the socially prescribed response blots out. If we say some soldiers behaved in a certain way we show them to the audience behaving in that way. The audience will not judge this as they would an account or description or claim. They will judge with the total involvement they use in their daily lives, with all their senses, with the subtle apprehensions with which they go about their daily business, the consciousness of the world which they validate with their self-consciousness. We shall give them tools of historical hind-sight and access to what is usually hidden, distorted or blurred. This can result in a development of understanding, an improved interpretation of the world, and so in a development of self-knowledge and self-consciousness. The audience cannot repeat itself. It is forced to reassess itself. Of course a dramatist can't prevent an audience from hardening its reaction. That's one reason why theatre can't by itself change the world. But if the audience decide that what we thought was true is false they will still have been changed, not merely for themselves but for society. Their views will have been increasingly identified and defined. So theatre can co-operate with all those who are in any way involved in rationally changing society and evolving a new consciousness. It may initiate the change in some people. What an audience says when it leaves a theatre is less important than what it thinks six months later. Some people angrily walk out of a theatre but six

months later know that the play was voicing views they had already started to accept.

Plays should deal, either comically or seriously, with situations, accounts and characters, which concern the audience in their daily life. But a dramatist need not always deal with the present. The past is also an institution owned by society. Our understanding of the past will change with our developing self-consciousness. This is not a partisan rewriting of history but a moral discovery of it. Our account of the past will be compared with other accounts. But the audience's comparison will be made in the sensitive way I have described. We cannot merely say that our account is correct. We must demonstrate it and prove it in the rationality of the stage.

Often the received image of the present, the consciousness of it, and so the corresponding self-consciousness, will not be a true interpretation of reality. Often the received interpretation is influenced, subverted, by the overt teaching and subtler persuasions of social institutions administering to the philosophy and needs of an obsolescent ruling class. Even if this were not so, human beings would still have to become involved in the active creation of their nature, since technology would always be disturbing their relationship to the environment and society. Certainly, in the present, we see ourselves and the world through class eyes: and the working class either sees the world and itself through its own class eyes (which means it is free to create a new culture and not merely produce the condition that requires a new culture) or it sees through the eyes of its masters, judges and other institutionalizers. Because of this, merely recounting an event or telling a story on stage will not provide the opportunity for a correct interpretation of the event or story or the people involved. These things may be misinterpreted, and often will be, because many of the audience will not be politically conscious and so will not understand the event or story or even the moral content of the language in which it is described or played. As we cannot merely tell stories or record events we have to handle punctured myths or broken stories. Effect no longer follows cause, judgement no

longer assesses deed, as they did in the past. Not even imagery works for us as it did in the past. Above all, moral language is caught in the same trap. So it is not easy for contemporary writers to contain experience and moral teaching in myths and stories in the way a more secure, settled society could. The way of telling a story, and the normative use of language, no longer contains an implicit interpretation. While we remain part of our present institutional societies our lives have no meaning and therefore stories about them have no meaning. Stories cannot present their own interpretation, can no longer teach us how they should be understood. The dramatist cannot confront the audience with truth by telling a story. The interpretation is counterfeited by society. Even the normative language we use to survive in capitalist society cannot be used to interpret it, our language is fouled by its involvement in that society just as morality is fouled by religion. This means that our moral sanity is at stake. Nor will a technical language of politics or sociology solve the problem because, although it can analyse realism, it cannot reproduce the appearance of reality on stage. And we certainly do not live in a society where the institutions are strong enough to criticize themselves – or rich enough. We are not like American capitalism, which could finance and profit from films on the wickedness of lynching blacks. It is simply that we have to rewrite human consciousness.

This is not a new problem in art – it has always been the task of art, but it has become a more urgent problem because changes in the technological basis of society and consciousness have become so extreme. When one considers the uproar, the sound and fury, of so much twentieth-century art, it is as if a child were trying to speak a new language. All art is a record of reality and an interpretation of it. If the interpretation is valid it changes naturalism into realism and so into art. Art does not consist in the recording or reproduction of a thing (that is merely one sort of skill) but in analysing what is recorded or reproduced. If we look at a painting of a bowl of flowers and ask what part of the painting is art, the

answer is not that art is the recording of the bowl and flowers, but is in the way they are recorded – that is, in the analysis or interpretation of them. This means, finally, that art is created by the human, social need to interpret experience and not merely passively submit to it. The equivalent of this in human consciousness is experience and the valid interpretation of it. A person of whom this is typical is cultured, and a work of art is something which helps to create this culture.

A human being incorporates his analysis of experience as part of his experience, and art which demonstrates its analysis in terms of what it records, rather than in externally originated comments on it, proves itself, and is usually more effective in deepening and strengthening human self-consciousness. Of course the artist may not always be able to choose. In a society that incorporates so little truth in its institutions and mores that it cannot reveal itself to itself in any way, how can an artist incorporate true conceptual knowledge into a *record* of that society? If he portrays the suffering of a beggar he may be told that thrift is a higher form of morality than pity. It might seem that the artist could then only comment from outside, in propaganda, and not reveal from within, in art. But there is always a working class which by its experience creates moral values and so this situation can never last long. Perhaps technology *could* be used to make it permanent, but this could only happen if the working class had been made hopelessly robot-like in its experience and responses, and history would then stand still.

It is useful to consider some of the techniques Brecht and other theatre workers used to overcome this difficulty. A scene can be interrupted by displaying placards that explain or comment on what happens in that scene. This helps the audience to understand what it is being shown and to see itself in a new light. And apart from the concepts or slogans on the placards there is also the vitalizing experience of seeing physically demonstrated the truth that life need not be an ungraspable flow of experience (to be understood only through pastiches of the past – as in Joyce's epic

Ulysses) but that new interpretations can be drawn from it. The physical demonstration of this in the theatre helps to create a new way of approaching experience outside the theatre. (At its simplest many people now even stick placards and posters on the walls of their homes.) But there is a limit to what this can achieve. It merely says that something is so and, even though it is in fact true, saying it does not test or prove it in the laboratory of art, in the rationality of the stage. If this were sufficient there would be no need for theatre.

Brecht also paid attention to the method of acting. He believed that a character should be shown not so much as an individual but as a class function. Perhaps there should be a difference between the way members of the exploiting class and the way others are shown. Members of the exploiting class deny their moral function, in practice, while claiming it institutionally. They have merely eccentricity – eccentricity is an attribute over-prized in dying cultures – taste, discretion, etiquette, style, collections of pictures, libraries and so forth. But working-class people create their humanity by daily experience of resistance or impulse for change. Their acts when they do this consciously are moral – and, incidentally, truly individual though united with others. But if a difference is made in the playing of the ruling class and this difference is merely a stage technique (caricature or masks, for example) and is not recorded from reality, then again the play's moral statements may not have been tested and proved – that is, turned into art – but merely assumed. The analysis of an event must not swamp the recording of it. We have to show the mask under the face not the mask on it. Perhaps we should show members of the ruling class in the way they see themselves: it is this good light which is so corrupting, so destructive in Western democracies, not least because it appropriates moral language. Of course, in open class war the role of the artist is clearer. The situation polarizes roles for everyone. But at the moment, in our society as it is, the truth is more terrible than the caricature of it. To show this truth, just as to show the mask under the face, we

need a new way of acting, one that will not simplify the complexities of experience by abstracting from it but will let us make the total complexity of a character simple and understandable. After all, that is what self-consciousness does when it develops into political consciousness, into class consciousness, in working people. Self-consciousness then becomes self-manipulative because it has then become a body of concepts, ideas, precepts, tests and experience which have been shown to be valid in critical, defining situations. If this insight and understanding could be used to develop a form of acting that could demonstrate truth to the audience, that would be the most important advance our theatre could make.

The dramatist can help to create a new theatre by the way he writes. He should dramatize not the story but the analysis. He will still have to present the story coherently, just as the painter must achieve a likeness, because that represents the experience, the anecdotal autobiography the audience brings to the theatre. But the scenes will not present the story in the way that is traditionally thought to be satisfying or coherent. In *The Bundle* I tried to find ways of dramatizing the analysis. The play is not best understood as a story of hero Wang but as a demonstration of how the words 'good' and 'bad', and moral concepts in general, work in society and how they ought to work if men are to live rationally with their technology, with nature and with one another. These are some of the moments in *The Bundle* when the analysis is dramatized: in scene seven, when Wang speaks calmly as the blood flows down his chin; at the end of scene five, in the play-within-the-play; in scene nine, the merchant's sudden animal shouts of 'Yu!' (these are shouts of terror, not abbreviations of 'You!'); at the end of scene three, Wang's choice of the word 'buy' when he shouts; in scene eight (c), the mother's struggle to move and her scream; and in scene eight (a), the use of the water bowl – at first this is an object in the story and then it is abstracted from the story and put into the analysis, when the ferryman with a calm, simple gesture places it on the ground and offers the audience an

elucidation, just as earlier he had offered Tiger the clear water. The changing of the bundle by the river from a baby in scenes one and four to rifles in scene eight (b) is also a dramatization of the analysis. The director, designer and actors must use such moments as dramatic high-points. They are not 'bits of business'.

The way a play is performed and the mise-en-scène designed teach the audience how to respond to the play and analyse it. Consider the man-handling of the boat in scene three. The boat not merely arrives, it is also removed. This man-handling would be clumsy in a well-made play. The well-made play deceives the audience into believing that the story will itself teach them how it should be interpreted. Instead, in this play the boat is carried out neatly and efficiently by the keepers (helped by the passengers if need be) so that it marks a pause in the play, preparing for the incident that must follow. It does not stop the play or become an incident interesting purely for itself (as Brecht might have been tempted to see it) but with tact and discretion it moves the play forward and teaches the audience their freedom in interpreting the play. Remember, the story will no longer interpret itself, as a joke can, or absolve the audience from the need to interpret it, as a myth might once have done. So the way the performers interpret the problems of performing the play can involve the audience in the interpretation of the meaning, the analysis, of the play.

Brecht sometimes suggests that each scene can be complete in itself and that this isolation of scenes can be used to interpret reality. But the connection between the scenes is essential because it is part of the analysis. Scenes cannot, it is true, relate to one another merely for the purposes of the story, because audiences can no longer passively interpret stories and so the dramatist cannot confront the audience with truth in this way. Instead, the choice and ordering of scenes is decided by the analysis – that is, the analysis will dictate the structure of the story; but care must be taken, as I have said, that it does not swamp it. Azdak the judge, in *The Caucasian Chalk Circle*, vanishes like a deus ex machina after showing that it is possible for judgement to be wise. This is done

by incidents in a scene. He does not stay to show that wisdom is practical. In *Cymbeline* a god descends so that we may understand (he tells us not to ask questions), and Azdak seems to vanish so that we may believe! For all his earthiness he is a voice shouting from an upper window, not someone we met in the street. Practicality can only be shown by the ordering of scenes, not by incidents in scenes. The epic's structure must have meaning – it is not a collection of scenes showing that meaning is logically possible. The epic must have a unity based on practical truth, just as once it was based on mythological coherence. This unity comes from the analysis, which demonstrates, embodies cause and effect in a coherent way. The scenes in *The Bundle* were chosen and ordered for this reason. Obvious examples are the parallels between scenes one and four; the placing of scene seven between scenes six and eight, where it interrupts the story, instead of before scene six; the decision to dramatize the preparation for the fight and the consequences of it and not the fight itself – which the traditonal story would have required (some critics were so confused by this that they thought the rifles were not used, although scene nine makes it clear they were).

The 'dramatization of the analysis instead of the story', in both the choice and ordering of the scenes and in the incidents dramatically emphasized in the scenes, is a way of reinstating meaning in literature. It may seem cold and abstract but it is not. The analysis can give us the beauty and vitality that once belonged to myth, without its compromises and intellectual reallocation of meaning. It can be the most exciting part of the play, dramatized through powerful images and dramatic confrontations between appearance and reality. But these dramatizations must not exist in their own right as dramatic effects. They demonstrate those crises in a story when the audience are asked to be not passive victims or witnesses, but interpreters of experience, agents of the future, restoring meaning to action by recreating self-consciousness. At these moments the audience are superior to the actors: they are on the real stage.

I have touched on several matters and not had time to discuss them fully. And it might seem that some of what I've said is too theoretical to be a guide to practical performance – but *this* is something I do not apologize for. We cannot know how to write, direct, design or act till we know why we have a stage. As a species we need an image of ourselves. Other animals are guided by instincts and protected by limited needs. We make decisions, and to do this wisely we need an image of ourselves, a human image. Our biology prepares us for this and if we do not create such an image we cannot use the opportunities of our technology without destroying or corrupting ourselves. Culture is created by a rational, self-manipulating self-consciousness. One of the means of creating this is art. All societies have used art. It is a biological requirement of the orderly functioning of human beings. But other societies have used art not in the way tired business-men want to use our theatre, to escape from labour which denies them self-respect and self-knowledge, but in order to learn how to live and work so that we may be happy and our moral concern for one another is not wasted.

EDWARD BOND
1978

The Bundle was first performed by the Royal Shakespeare Company at the Warehouse Theatre, London. The production opened on 13 January 1978 with the following cast:

FERRYMAN	Bob Peck
BASHO	Patrick Stewart
WANG	Mike Gwilym
FIRST KEEPER	Rod Culbertson
SECOND KEEPER	Alfred Molina
OLD MAN	Clyde Pollitt
OLD WOMAN	Judith Harte
FERRYMAN'S WIFE	Margaret Ashcroft
PU-TOI	Kevin O'Shea
LU	Lynda Rooke
KUNG-TU	John Nettles
WOMAN	Meg Davies
TIGER	Paul Moriarty
SHEOUL	Francis Viner
KAKA	Greg Hicks
TOR-QUO	Martin Read
WATER SELLER 1	Kevin O'Shea
WATER SELLER 2	Greg Hicks
CRACKER MAN	Martin Read
SOLDIER 1	Rod Culbertson
SOLDIER 2	Alfred Molina
HUSBAND	Christopher Whitehouse
SOLDIER 3	Christopher Whitehouse
TO-SI	Christopher Whitehouse
SAN-KO	Alfred Molina
GOW	Rod Culbertson
TUAN (Corpse)	Michael Townsend

Directed by Howard Davies
Designed by Chris Dyer
Lighting by David Boshell

Part One

ONE

Fenland. A river and a river bank in the fens. A bell on a post. A baby left by the river.

FERRYMAN. I ask why the reverend sir sets out so early in the morning. He is not a soldier or a tax collector.

BASHO. The landowner wanted to make me judge of the fenland villages. I answered: not worthy. I have seen the darkness of human life – murder theft death. The *truth* when it is dark corrupts. First I must find enlightenment. Then I will judge. The landowner said: when the old judge dies our court will be empty. Don't seek enlightenment too long. I said: I seek till I find.

FERRYMAN. Will the reverend sir now say what enlightenment is?

BASHO. All creation seeks enlightenment as this river flows to the sea. Does the river ask: what is the way? Men are a dark river. We get and spend, fret and eddy, twist into whirlpools till the water seems to devour itself in its frenzy – we delay. See where the river flows to its mouth and enters the ocean, where the great earth sees the vision of itself in the sky and turns to water. (FERRYMAN *helps* BASHO *from the boat.*) May your life prosper.

FERRYMAN. The reverend sir hasn't paid the ferryman.

BASHO. I go to be reborn. Does the midwife charge the child? Is your life so useful, your soul full of such brightness, your trade done with such courtesy – that you can charge enlightenment a penny on its journey into the world?

FERRYMAN. The reverend sir knows our life is hard, there are so few travellers –

BASHO. For those who suffer there is grace.

FERRYMAN. Grace without food won't help me to row my boat.

BASHO. Not one penny. Will you tell the keeper of heaven: 'Yes, I charged the saints a penny to travel in my boat. I come empty-handed, clothed in sin. Let me enter.' You ask me to damn your immortal soul. (*Sees child.*) A child. Left by the river. These villages are in hell! You see why I seek enlightenment. (*To child.*) Why were you left here?

FERRYMAN. The parents were too poor to feed it.

BASHO. They threw you out to die.

FERRYMAN. They laid it by the river and prayed to heaven that passengers would take pity on it. Take the child on your journey!

BASHO. Take the child! I have to cross mountains where there are tigers. Crawl through swamps – unless someone loves know-ledge enough to carry me on his back. Beg – and go without. You take it.

FERRYMAN. We're as poor as its parents. And our house is an ignorant place. With the reverend sir the child would grow wise and good. People will take pity on him if he has a child.

BASHO. Ah . . . No. Knowledge must be loved for itself. I would be like an organ grinder with a monkey on his back. If the child had been big it could have carried my bundle. Then heaven's purpose would have been clear. No, it was put here to tempt me at the start of my journey. Shall the sage turn back and never get further than his doorstep? Child, I am Basho the great seventeenth-century poet. I brought the haiku to perfection. Listen!

> The saints' feet are hands
> Washing the dusty earth
> On the narrow road
> That leads to enlightenment

I am often asked to recite that. Of course you understand nothing yet. But my words are a blessing. Child we are both by the river at the start of our journey. Yours may end at this river. I shall cross many rivers. Neither you nor I has a coin to

pay the ferryman or lay on our eyes. Learn to be patient. Would the sky alter by one tear if I took you with me? Does the ant on the mountain ask the pines why they sigh? One can take nothing into the mirror of eternity but the vision of oneself.

BASHO *goes. The* FERRYMAN *stands by his boat and looks at the child.*

FERRYMAN. In my house you'd be hungry. Wake up at night with the cold. And I'm not a good man. My wife wouldn't be able to save you from my wicked temper. Wicked. Sometimes I wait all day and no one comes. On those evenings I couldn't stand your crying – though I was crying myself. If you'd dropped off the back of a carriage the lackey (*Starts poling.*) would have been sent to pick you up. The coachman would have been flogged for jolting. You're a poor man's child – you must learn to understand. Be grateful to your parents. Look at the good cloth you're wrapped in! They could have sold that and lived like lords. Your mother didn't have a cloth to dry her eyes. She looked down at you and said: 'Now the cradle clothes are a shroud.' Yes, well. You have much to understand and forgive. The poet was right: patience.

A curlew calls. The FERRYMAN *stops.*

There'd be no harm in making sure you're properly wrapped. (*He starts to punt back to the child.*) You could have kicked your clothes loose. Or they could be too tight. Your parents didn't want to hurt you. I owe it to them to look. You're not crying. It can't be too bad. Perhaps the worst's already over. It would be wrong to wake you. I'll just straighten your clothes.

The FERRYMAN *gets out of the boat, goes to the child and arranges its wrapping.*

I won't pick you up. Better not. I'll tell my passengers: a little boy. A mouth to feed now, two hands to work later. Sow in spring, eat in winter. (*He goes back to the boat.*) Whoever gets

you's in luck. They'll fight over you. Heaven must have meant you for someone better than me. If I took you I'd be stealing from the gods. This is the passenger bell. (*He rings one note on the bell.*) They ring and I come. I help them into the boat. Young and old, rich and poor, innocent and some so guilty the river couldn't wash them clean. I take them all across. That is the bell.

The FERRYMAN *gets into the boat and begins to pole.*

We have no children. Heaven was kind. It knew we couldn't feed them. When you welcome us to heaven you'll understand why I left you. You'll be young and happy for ever, we'll be old and soiled.

The curlew calls. The FERRYMAN *stops rowing.*

Terrible to be poor. We have nothing and the world is a mouth wide open saying: 'Give!' We must be hard to live. Yet at any moment a curlew can call and we are lost.

The FERRYMAN *poles back to the child.*

God knows what my wife will say. I'll leave you outside the door where she'll find you. Then she'll be guilty. Or say a god came walking over the water as brazen as anything and when I lifted my hands to cover my face – you were dropped in them – Tch! She'd box my ears! No supper tonight. She'll say: 'If I feed this I can't feed you.'

The FERRYMAN *picks up the child.*

This is a bad thing. Not a wise one. We throw kindness around as if we were kings. Yes, I shall eat tonight – I must be strong to work. So I have taken my wife's bread. She'll go without every night. Soon she'll grow weak. Her life will be half a life. She's shared my sorrow for years. I love her. Yet I betray her for love for you. I kill her. (*Poles.*) Where is the wisdom in that? If you understood you'd be shocked. Look, I row gently so that you

sleep there on the floor of my boat. Your fingers lie on your chest like chips from a gravestone. I must hope you're dead. Or you die in the crossing. Then all I need do is dig your grave. That would be best. We'd be spared the results of this folly. Where is the wisdom in that?

TWO

The same. Night. Fourteen years later. The FERRYMAN *fishes from the boat.* WANG *sits by the shaded lamp.*

WANG. It's not our boat.

FERRYMAN. Not now.

WANG. Why not?

FERRYMAN. It went in taxes.

WANG. Why?

FERRYMAN. No money. So few passengers.

WANG. Why?

FERRYMAN. Robbers. People don't like to travel.

WANG (*after a slight silence*). The wind ruffles my sleeve like the water. What are taxes?

FERRYMAN. Taxes make sure the country's well run.

WANG. Father –

FERRYMAN. Sh!

WANG. But . . .

FERRYMAN (*after a slight silence*). I'll try to explain. It's true: the other day I got this cut on my head. I took two hefty young men in the boat. They said they were going to join the emperor's army. What a pleasure for an old man to row two strong young men to their glory. In the middle of the stream they laughed and said: 'Give us the takings.' I said: 'Boys, you're my only passengers this week and so far you've given me nothing.' Then because they were angry and because they wanted to amuse

themselves, they said: 'Let's sink the boat.' I said: 'Boys, this boat is the landowner's.' Their whole manner changed. If the boat had been mine they'd have sunk it. With so many robbers about the police have many more important things to protect than us. But if they'd sunk the landowner's boat they'd have been hunted down to the ends of China. So, that's taxes: the soldiers left me the boat and only cracked my head . . . Sh.

WANG. No insects on the lamp. Cold.

FERRYMAN (*half sighs*). I wanted to catch a fish for your mother.

WANG. Who owns the river?

FERRYMAN. You're keeping the fish away.

WANG. Who owns the fish?

FERRYMAN. What fish?

WANG. Why do we fish at night?

FERRYMAN. The landowner owns the river and the fish. We can't afford a licence to fish.

WANG. So we steal the fish.

FERRYMAN (*slight pause*). I will try to explain. The landowner owns the boat and the river and the fish. You could say he owns us – he owns the only way we can live. In return he keeps us safe. (*Wang moves as if to interrupt.*) Wait! You sit on the bank in the sun and wave your arms to keep off the insects. Some still bite – but not many. Well, if the landowner didn't keep the robbers away they'd come down the chimney and take the food out of your mouth! We're his property. It's in his interest to look after us. There.

WANG. We steal the fish to stay alive to pay taxes so that there'll be no more stealing and the –

FERRYMAN. I often wonder who your father was. A priest – or philosopher – or a footpad. I think you –

The ferry bell rings, sharp and clear in the dark. Immediately WANG *douses the light.*

FERRYMAN (*faking his voice to sound as if it came from the far bank*). Who's there – so late?

BASHO. Basho.

FERRYMAN. Basho? . . . O reverend sir, one moment!

Splashing as the boat is poled towards the shore. The lamp is lit.

Is it really the reverend sir?

BASHO. Am I known? My fame goes before. I've walked through a thousand valleys and climbed to the top of the world, crossed so many rivers and watched the pole strike the water a million times. My journey has lasted fourteen years. They seem like fourteen lifetimes.

As the boat approaches the light falls on BASHO. *He is old and tired and dirty. His feet are bound in lumps of rag.*

Tap tap tap through China. I've worn out seventeen walking sticks. My feet are bound with rags! I picked them out of the rubbish in the corner of a grave-yard. They'd been used to bind corpses' mouths. Ferryman, is this the way to the deep north?

FERRYMAN. This is your village.

BASHO. My village?

FERRYMAN. Yes reverend sir.

BASHO. My village? This is my village?

FERRYMAN. Yes reverend sir.

The FERRYMAN *steps from his boat and goes to take* BASHO's *arm to help him into the boat.* WANG *holds the light so that it falls on the* FERRYMAN's *face.*

Welcome!

BASHO. This is a dream!

FERRYMAN. No reverend sir, I am the ferryman –

BASHO (*turning round in a circle*). I've taken the wrong road. Walked in a circle. I must go back. Where is the road to the deep north? (*Faces the* FERRYMAN *again.*) Where? Where?

FERRYMAN (*goes to help him, takes his arm to lead him to the boat*). But reverend sir, be comforted!

BASHO (*striking him off*). Get off! A vision sent by the devil! Get off! This is the king of the dead!

> BASHO *falls in a faint.*

FERRYMAN. Water! He's fainted! The poor old man!

> WANG *sets the lamp on the ground, fetches water from the river and throws it in* BASHO's *face.* BASHO *comes round spluttering.*

BASHO. . . what? . . .

> BASHO *faints again.*

FERRYMAN. He's fainted again! Water! Quick!

> WANG *fetches water from the river.*

WANG. Who is he?

> WANG *throws water in* BASHO's *face.* BASHO *comes round.*

BASHO. The water! Enlightenment!

FERRYMAN. Sir?

BASHO. Enlightenment. The water on my face . . . Enlightenment! I have enlightenment! The meaning of my journey! – heaven has shown me the mirror on my doorstep! Enlightenment!

WANG (*to* FERRYMAN) . . . What is enlightenment?

BASHO (*kneels*).

> I travelled the earth
> To the gateway of heaven
> Who kept the door? Doubt!
> How many turn back
> At the last

Help me.

> FERRYMAN *helps* BASHO *to his feet.* WANG *watches.*

WANG. What is enlightenment?

FERRYMAN. Yes, sir, teach us!

BASHO. I crawled over China like a fly on the back of a mirror. I

reached the bright silver river at the edge. The glass cuts. That is the moment the crowd turns back. I crossed the river. Now I am on the other side, on the mirror of eternity. Every pillar in the temple sees the altar from its own angle. The sun dazzles from afar, those who live on it see by its light. I have found the little stone that holds the laws of the world in your hand.

FERRYMAN. Sir –?

BASHO. Do not ask for enlightenment till you're ready to lose all. I look into the mirror of this river. If this mirror appeared in your boat – a little round hole in the bottom – you would block it out –

FERRYMAN. Sir!

BASHO. You do not seek enlightenment.

FERRYMAN. But for Wang? This is the boy who was left by the river.

BASHO (*not remembering*). Left by the river . . . ?

TWO KEEPERS *jump out of the darkness.*

SECOND KEEPER. Ha!

FIRST KEEPER. Ho!

SECOND KEEPER. Got you!

FIRST KEEPER. At last!

SECOND KEEPER. Red handed!

FIRST KEEPER. Where's the fish?

SECOND KEEPER (*going to search*). In the boat!

FIRST KEEPER (*grabbing* BASHO). What's this?

SECOND KEEPER. Three! Buyer from town!

BASHO. Leave me alone!

FERRYMAN. Sirs this is Basho the poet.

BASHO. My arm.

FIRST KEEPER. Where's the fish?

SECOND KEEPER. In the bush.

FIRST KEEPER. I'll arm you!

FERRYMAN. Sirs this is the poet from our village. (*To* BASHO.) Reverend sir don't be angry. They were boys when you left.

SECOND KEEPER. Is he a poet? Throw him in the water and see if he shouts alas!

BASHO. At the moment of enlightenment
          The devil springs
          What is knowledge
          Except that the world is evil!

The landowner's made me a judge. If ruffians like you protect the law – it's time I came back.

The TWO KEEPERS *go a little to one side.*

FIRST KEEPER. Poachers don't talk like that.

SECOND KEEPER. There's nothing in the bush.

FIRST KEEPER. No harm in stepping careful.

The TWO KEEPERS *go back to the others.*

FIRST KEEPER. Sir, we're sorry we frightened you.

BASHO. My arm!

SECOND KEEPER. There are a lot of bad people in these parts.

FIRST KEEPER. In the dark – we can't take risks. The floods are bad. Every harvest is spoiled. The young men run off to the swamps and turn into bandits and poachers.

BASHO. It's almost broken!

SECOND KEEPER. We try to do our duty and carry out the will of heaven, as it says in our oath.

FIRST KEEPER. Not easy these days. A judge will understand.

SECOND KEEPER (*picks up the rod from the ground*). What's . . .! A fishing rod!

WANG. Walking stick. I cut it for the poet. His is worn out.

FIRST KEEPER. So! We meet a poet and a saint all in one night!

FERRYMAN. We heard the bell. So late – we knew it would be urgent. So we hurried.

BASHO. Take me home.

The TWO KEEPERS *watch* WANG *and the* FERRYMAN *help* BASHO *into the boat.*

THREE

The village burial hills. Refugees camp among the gravestones. They are near the limits of exhaustion. They wear rags. On the ground: bundles, and a cooking pot over a dead fire.

FERRYMAN, *his* WIFE, LU (*a young girl*), PU-TOI (*a young farmer*), KUNG-TU (*a middle-aged shopkeeper*) *an* OLD MAN *and an* OLD WOMAN.

Quiet.

OLD MAN. It's six days.

OLD WOMAN. The flood should have gone down.

OLD MAN. It always goes after six days.

OLD WOMAN. Even four.

OLD MAN (*cries*). That's all the rice we could bring. No one could help us.

OLD WOMAN. The landowner won't let us starve, brother.

The OLD WOMAN *beckons the* FERRYMAN *to one side.*

OLD MAN. All this water.

PU-TOI. That'll take days to go down.

OLD WOMAN (*aside to* FERRYMAN). Did you get the rice?

FERRYMAN (*shakes his head*). I have to steal it from our bundle in the night. Wang was awake.

OLD WOMAN. You promised.

OLD MAN. The water's been on the edge of Kan's grave six days. Just by the little hole. Like a cat waiting to pounce.

OLD WOMAN. We'll starve.

FERRYMAN. We're all hungry.

OLD WOMAN. Our rice won't last two days.

FERRYMAN. I'll try tonight. Wang would be angry if he knew I'm feeding you. His mother's weak, she needs the rice . . .

OLD WOMAN. See my wrists! So thin.

FERRYMAN. He sleeps with the bundle by his head. Please – don't cry, my dear. I'll try.

LU. We shouldn't camp out here on the graves. I have a bad dream.

PU-TOI. This is the only high land.

WANG. There's the landowner's hill!

OLD WOMAN. What d'you dream?

LU. I'm asleep on our grave. I fall in – and there's my house! The room, the mat, the bowl with the copper rivets, even the broom in the corner. But no window or door. Then a fly comes in through the wall – and I know I'm dead: flies are buzzing in and out of me.

> OLD WOMAN *groans.*

WANG. A boat!

> *They all look off.*

OLD MAN. A boat!

LU. Look!

PU-TOI. They're coming to get us.

FERRYMAN (*to his wife*). Our boat's coming.

OLD MAN. Hush! We mustn't shout.

> *They wave, collect their bundles and form into a queue on the edge of the water.*

OLD WOMAN. Our houses are still under water.

OLD MAN. The landowner will take us in.

PU-TOI. He'll let us sleep in the compound.

VOICES (*off*). Here! Here! Here!

LU. They're all shouting!

OLD MAN (*yells*). No respect for the dead!

PU-TOI. We'd better shout! (*Calls.*) Here! Here!

ALL. Help us! Help us!

LU (*calls*). Old people here!

PU-TOI (*calls*). And a sick woman! Help!

KUNG-TU (*calls*). Us first! Us first!

VOICES (*off, calling*). Us first. Here. A woman's giving birth. Don't let her bear her child in the graveyard. She'll defile the graves. Help! Help!

OLD MAN. No use shouting. They'll go where they want. Kneel. (*He, the* OLD WOMAN *and* LU *kneel.*) Ancestors I thank you for sharing your resting place –

VOICES (*off, calling*). Help. Help.

OLD MAN. We hope we haven't troubled your sleep –

WANG (*calls*). Here!

OLD MAN. My dear wife . . .

OLD WOMAN (*to* OLD MAN). Sh now.

OLD MAN (*in tears*). I've slept by you again with my head on this ground . . .

OLD WOMAN. Hush.

OLD MAN. Every year I pay the interest on your medicine. I don't begrudge it. It's a happiness to me to pay for what you had. Soon I'll be too old to live. I'll come and sleep by your side. What happiness . . .

OLD WOMAN (*weeps silently*). My brother's an old fool. Crying when the boat's coming!

VOICES (*off, calling*). Over here! Us! Help!

PU-TOI (*to* FERRYMAN). It's your boat! (*Calls.*) Us! It's our boat!

FERRYMAN. When the water rose the landowner commandeered it. It's coming here first.

PU-TOI (*calls and waves*). Here! Here!

WANG. Mother. They'll take us to the landowner's compound. We'll build a shelter against the wall. His stone wall's so high the floor's dry even when it rains. If we lived here instead of letting the dead have it –

OLD MAN (*to* FERRYMAN). Keep your boy quiet! We only live a short life. Even at my age after all I've seen it looks short. When we die we're here for ever. What respect is it when we can't house the dead – who need it most! No wonder the flood's

lasted six days. Our village! – swearing, lying, profaning, thieving! – no wonder heaven's not kind! You young people – I shudder at what will happen to us when we're dead. You'll throw us out on the fields.

FERRYMAN (*calmingly*). The boat's coming.

OLD MAN. The village saint speaks!

OLD WOMAN (*waving to the boat*). A grandmother blesses you!

PU-TOI (*to* LU). Ask Kung-tu to pay your fare. He sleeps on his bundle at night. Not comfortable – that hard lump in the back.

KUNG-TU. If I had money would I be on this pauper ground? I'd be buried higher up. With trees.

OLD MAN *and* OLD WOMAN *giggle.*

PU-TOI (*laughs*). Kung-tu scrimps and saves but he has to come and pay his respects with the poor where his ancestors are.

OLD WOMAN (*giggles*). Paupers' graves.

OLD MAN. When he's very rich he'll dig them up –

OLD WOMAN. Dig up the bones!

OLD MAN. – and bury them in rich ground. He can't afford to yet.

OLD WOMAN. The priest would want a lot of money.

OLD MAN. You might need a bishop for that.

They giggle.

KUNG-TU. I work – and you sit and jeer –

The others laugh.

Till you're in trouble! Then you know the value of money!

The TWO KEEPERS *pole in the boat.*
All the people on the mound bow. The KEEPERS *land the boat on the hill. The* SECOND KEEPER *ties it up to a gravestone. The* OLD MAN *and* OLD WOMAN *come forward.*

OLD WOMAN (*crying as the boat arrives*). Bless them. Bless them. I couldn't have come through another night. At my age you –

FIRST KEEPER. The dead must have thought this lot were ghosts come to haunt them!

SECOND KEEPER. How much?

OLD MAN. We left our money behind.

OLD WOMAN. The flood came so fast. We ran to the graveyard. The water was –! (*Points to her waist.*)

SECOND KEEPER. That bundle.

OLD MAN. It's all we've got. The rest was washed away.

OLD WOMAN (*undoing the bundle*). Two mats, three bowls, chop sticks.

SECOND KEEPER. That!

OLD MAN (*pretending not to understand what the* KEEPER *wants*). This leather belt? It'll last me out. It stays on me because I'm old. Young man on the go like you: snap straight away.

SECOND KEEPER (*bored at the* OLD MAN's *pathetic attempts at evasion*). No, that!

OLD MAN. Take the belt and leave me the padded jacket. At your age you don't know how cruel the wind is. I must keep my jacket.

OLD WOMAN. I share it with my brother at night.

KUNG-TU. They'll go on to the next hill!

OLD WOMAN. Brother?

OLD MAN (*takes coins from the jacket lining*). All I've got. Don't drop it, it's slippery with years of sweat.

The SECOND KEEPER *takes the coins.*

FIRST KEEPER. And the coat.

OLD MAN. No.

SECOND KEEPER. Two fares! We can take a trip round the grave-stones while you think.

KUNG-TU. You old fools! They'll take the lot if we freeze to death!

The OLD MAN *hands over the coat. The* OLD MAN *and* OLD WOMAN *get into the boat.*

OLD MAN. May your ancestors judge.

SECOND KEEPER. Old people fall out of boats like babies falling out of cradles.

OLD WOMAN (*to* OLD MAN). Hush. (*To* SECOND KEEPER.) You'll get old too.

FIRST KEEPER. Too wicked. Our throats'll be cut long before. Don't begrudge us. You've had more out of life than we'll ever get.

SECOND KEEPER (*to* FERRYMAN). For three.

FERRYMAN (*bows*). I know that ferrymen have to live. (*Gestures off*.) Look at the crowd! The boat will be heavy. How many trips? Let Wang and me work our passage.

VOICES (*off, crying*). What's happening? Get in the boat! Help! Be quick!

> KUNG-TU *steps forward*.

KUNG-TU. These fools will argue all day. I've got nothing here. Between us: I'm half-way into a deal. Rape seed left over from my neighbour. Safe in the waterproof jars. The moment the town merchant pays up I'll see you're –

FIRST KEEPER. Did he keep you awake counting coins?

SECOND KEEPER. No – his gold teeth were chattering.

FIRST KEEPER. If this water ever goes down you'll be crawling home with your arse in the mud. We'll be there first – and dig up your floors.

SECOND KEEPER. His face is so blank it could be on the side of a coin.

KUNG-TU. Bandits!

VOICES (*crying, off*). Us! Us! Us! Us! Us! Us!

FIRST KEEPER. Don't call us names. You're not so rich – yet – you can make the laws. Between us: you'll get your money's worth. Think of your mud floors tomorrow. You can't arrest everyone with an ugly face and a spade. We can. (KUNG-TU *hands over a roll of notes*.) Give him the chair!

KUNG-TU. No, no. That sort of show isn't –

SECOND KEEPER. The chair! He paid!
FIRST KEEPER. Respectable people must be respected.

> KUNG-TU *sits uncomfortably in the chair in the middle of the boat.*

> Pu-toi, farmer by day, by night fetches and carries for merchants in town. We haven't asked what. But it must pay – at those hours!

> PU-TOI *hands over money and steps silently into the boat.*

(*To* KUNG-TU.) That's how the town merchants get on. They employ deaf and dumb.
LU (*hand out to* KUNG-TU). Please. My money's at –
KUNG-TU. Don't ask me! They've got it! – Ha! They'll pay *you*.
(FIRST KEEPER. That sort of brute would hit her with this (*fist*) and drag her behind the graves where your latrine is. FIRST KEEPER *takes the hat from* KUNG-TU.) That pays for her.

> LU *steps into the boat. She's unsure who to thank.*

LU (*to the* KEEPERS). Thank you. (*To the* OLD MAN *and* OLD WOMAN.) Thank you. (*To* KUNG-TU.) Thank you.
FERRYMAN. We have these clothes –
WANG. It's our boat!
FERRYMAN. Quiet.
VOICES (*off, crying*). Help. Help. Quick. The woman's giving birth. The hill's slipping into the mud. The gravestones are falling over.

> *The* WOMAN *is heard in labour. Slowly during the scene the shouting, moaning, and sobbing increase to a climax and then fade into the hum, whimpering and stray cries of a desperate crowd.*

FERRYMAN. – three rice bowls, a cooking pot, a kettle, two mats, a mattress and cover for my wife. She rests her head on my legs. Leave us something to live on.

SECOND KEEPER (*pokes at bundle*). Soiled. Dirty old rubbish.

FIRST KEEPER. That cow's rats'-bane will be into everything. Don't touch them.

SECOND KEEPER. Their rags peel off like paint.

KUNG-TU. I've paid for my trip. Let's go! Isn't there anything you want?

FIRST KEEPER. Yes.

WANG. Then what?

FIRST KEEPER. We need consent.

FERRYMAN. What is it?

FIRST KEEPER. The son.

FERRYMAN. My son?

FIRST KEEPER. A proper indenture. Drawn up in a lawyer's office. A form of a loan. You get him back.

KUNG-TU. I did it to help my neighbour who went bankrupt. (*To* FERRYMAN.) Do your boy good. Needs controlling.

FERRYMAN. But who'll work the ferry when I'm old? We invested so much in him. If you take him away our lives have been wasted!

SECOND KEEPER. You'll survive. You have so far.

WANG. We'll live out here on the gravestones. Let the landowner be ashamed!

FERRYMAN. Quiet.

FIRST KEEPER. He couldn't keep quiet at his own funeral.

SECOND KEEPER. Nasty little bastard. Insulting, stealing . . .

VOICES (*off, crying*). Help!

SECOND KEEPER (*shouting off to the crowd*). Tell her if she drops the kid we'll charge the fare.

FERRYMAN (*to* WANG). You owe your life to us. Your mother can't stay here another night. Give her a little time.

WANG. I'm not a slave.

PU-TOI. I am. I slave day and night. We all do. What's it matter

if they call us a slave for once? That old woman's not worth taking. She'll be back in a few weeks. Let them stay – they won't have to pay for the trip to the grave-yard.

KUNG-TU. Confucius placed filial piety over all virtues. I shall remove my ancestors. They're not staying in this company.

WANG. He's not my father.

PU-TOI. All the more reason to thank him.

FERRYMAN. A year.

SECOND KEEPER. Ten.

FERRYMAN. No, no. Too long. I won't ask that. We'd never see him again. No not ten years.

OLD MAN. Who knows the wheel of his fate?

WANG. Two years.

FIRST KEEPER. Ten.

WANG. Three. No more. I'm fit. I'll do ten years work in three.

WIFE (*crying and holding* WANG's *hand*). It's wrong to take a young life, but I don't want to die and leave your father without me. (*She strokes his hand.*) Wang forgive me. You men in the boat: four. No more.

VOICES (*off, crying*). Help. Help. We're drowning. The graves are falling into the water.

SECOND KEEPER. Ten.

FERRYMAN (*squats*). It's over. We stay. The water will go down soon.

SECOND KEEPER. Why d'you think we're here? (*Points.*) Look!

LU. That uprooted tree. The water's started to flow.

PU-TOI. Yes! The water's running in white lines!

FIRST KEEPER. Would we waste time collecting you garbage if the water was falling and you could crawl home? The banks higher up have broken! The water will rise!

KUNG-TU. He's right! It's running into the hole by Kan's grave.

OLD WOMAN (*points off*). Look, it's stirring the branches of the trees.

OLD MAN (*trying to see*). My eyes!

OLD WOMAN. There!

LU. I thought they were hands coming out of the water!

OLD MAN. Where?

The shouting increases again, off.

PU-TOI. The whole landscape's moving – running –

KUNG-TU. Pushing the trees and the debris along with it.

The people in the boat suddenly lurch.

OLD MAN. The boat's beginning to move.

OLD WOMAN (*whimpering*). Brother! I'm frightened!

KUNG-TU. Pu-toi, you've got money. Ten years: six to one. Nine: five to two. Lu, you've got money at home. Five years: evens.

PU-TOI (*passes money*). Eight to three.

KUNG-TU. What it is to be young.

VOICES (*off*). Help us!

OLD MAN. Could you accept this bowl?

OLD WOMAN. Brother!

OLD MAN. It's a certainty. (KUNG-TU *takes cup. To the* OLD WOMAN.) It'll help us so much later on.

FIRST KEEPER. Wang, your last chance.

KUNG-TU. If only I hadn't worn my hat! Dressing up for a flood! I get these colds in my head.

FIRST KEEPER. It's wrong to force a bargain in hard times. Nine years. Not a second less.

WANG. No.

FIRST KEEPER. I once saw a herd of cattle outside a slaughter-house shoving to see who got in first.

The SECOND KEEPER *unropes the boat from the gravestone.*

OLD MAN *and*

OLD WOMAN. Goodbye.

PU-TOI (*to* KUNG-TU). It's not over.

The boat goes. FERRYMAN *holds his wife.* WANG *stands a little apart from them, rooted to the spot. The* WIFE *cries quietly.*

FERRYMAN. Don't cry my dear. We knew our lives would end. We have each other. Wang, swim.

WANG. No.

FERRYMAN. What is the use? Swim!

WANG. I'll stay.

FERRYMAN. These aren't your graves! You have no ancestors! Swim! Leave us together.

WIFE. If only . . .

WANG. I'm not a slave!

FERRYMAN. Swim! I order you!

WANG. The water will go down.

FERRYMAN. It's rising.

VOICES (*crying off*). Help. Help. The woman has given birth! I'm up to my neck in mud. Bodies are being washed out of the ground. The dead are floating round us. The landscape is moving.

FERRYMAN. You owe us nothing. We're not your parents. I was wrong to ask. I took you from the water: now you can swim!

WIFE. If only . . . If only . . .

WANG. Mother!

FERRYMAN. She's too weak to answer!

WANG (*stands stiffly, rooted to the spot. Yells*). Buy me! Buy me! Buy me!

The FERRYMAN *embraces his wife with one hand, reaches with the other towards* WANG *and then reaches it up as if holding off the sky. He cries. His wife embraces him.*

FERRYMAN. We're going to be saved! Saved!

WIFE. Our son. He saves us.

FERRYMAN. Our son.

WANG (*as before, yelling desperately*). Buy me! Buy me! Buy me!

FOUR

Another part of the river and the bank. An abandoned child.

BASHO *comes on and glances briefly. Calls back off-stage left.*

BASHO. It's quiet by the river. Here, in the shade of this tree. Fetch my court list from the carriage.

> BASHO *lays his cushion on the ground, sits, unfolds his travelling desk and writes.*

> > Bamboos flutter by the moorhen's nest
> > Army banners!
> > She does not ask
> > Where the river goes
> > Nor where the arrow flies

Slight pause. BASHO *glances surreptitiously off left and then writes again, slightly raising his voice so that it can be overheard by someone waiting quite near.*

> > The poet's brush
> > Made from hair tugged from his beard
> > Is dipped in black ink
> > He writes
> > The ink drains on the page
> > The brush turns grey

(*Calls left.*) Wang.

> WANG *comes on. He wears a servant's coat.*

Thank you. (*He takes the court list from* WANG. *Reads it.*) I called for water in the night. You were not there.
WANG. I visited my home.
BASHO. Is your mother well?
WANG. Better.

BASHO. You took her more food.

WANG. Yes.

BASHO. And the man you call father?

WANG. He's glad my mother's better.

BASHO (*reads the court list*). Mrs Su-tan broke her neighbour's arm because she stole her thatch – and sang at night. The neighbour came round, screamed in the street and threw stones through Su-tan's door. Su-tan's husband held the neighbour's broken arm while Su-tan broke the fingers on it. Such acts of human nature are so bestial, the times so dark, that it is not possible to see what we can do to help ourselves or change the times. They say your father is good.

WANG. He shelters travellers at home when they're too poor for the inn. He lets the sick cross for nothing, even in famine. He saved me from the river.

BASHO. A tree has one good fruit on it. Heaven smiled when he was born. You were there when I went to seek enlightenment. You were there again when I found it. The landowner gave you to me for a servant. We call the plans of heaven coincidence. Your nine years end today.

> WANG *is silent*.

> The arm of the woman who sang at night
> Was broken by angry neighbours
> She stands in my court
> And I wonder:
> Why do the poor sing?

Wang, I have taught you to write and how to study the classics. Your hands are pale from holding a pen. You stand behind my chair in court. You sit by the wall while poets sing to the koto. How can you work in the fields – or the shops? You can't live on the ferry. That supports two at most. Stay in my house. (*Pause.*) No gratitude?

WANG. Thank you. I can't stay.

BASHO (*writes*).

No bird flies as fast as the arrow
No fruit falls as straight as the axe
No man escapes his end
Or the road to it

Not as a servant the master's so used to he treats him as a friend in order to keep him as a servant. What torments you? The past? Even your parents couldn't say you were their child. So many babies are left by the river. How could they know even the day they left you? All trace is gone.

WANG. I don't ask those questions. It would be foolish.

BASHO. Then stay and seek peace.

WANG. No.

BASHO. The father first learns he has spoiled his child when his child tells him. Why did the woman break her neighbour's fingers? You forget that your eyes can ache with cold, the grit that comes in your mouth when you starve, the thin dirt on the rice bowl, filth decaying in corners, the smell of unwashed clothes. You can be too tired to clean and too hopeless to think. Such people are always lost, even at home. One day you may scream on the street and break your neighbour's bones. Ignorance destroys from within. Nothing is seen, but one day you collapse – mind and body.

I turned away from this world. I administer law for the good of heaven not the good of man. There's no help I can give to those so poor they can only seek self. They must live in ignorance – just as a stone must fall. You shared my house for nine years. If I could care for anything in this world it would be you. Stay.

WANG. No.

BASHO. Madmen take pleasure in destroying themselves.

WANG (*he has already seen the child upstage. He points*). Look, a child left by the river.

BASHO *turns his head to look.*

BASHO. Every day now. More and more. A whole generation left by the river. Dead?

WANG. No. It stirred a moment ago. Take it.

BASHO. How strange. For a moment I see into heaven. Once before – a child by the river. I left it to seek enlightenment. Now this child. What should we seek this time? Always enlightenment. Heaven has done this. You take the child. Live with it in my house. Then you will find the way.

WANG. There's no argument I can use. I've waited behind you in court and heard the innocent and the guilty plead. Living women with fingers twisting like ghosts, old men staring like lost children, murderers who laughed over corpses. I marvelled at them as they talked. How subtle the human mind is. Each told the truth in his way, even against himself. How strange their lives, the stories of the little things that shaped them. You can go for a walk, and come back another man. But you talk of the way as if it was laid down in an iron map. You must leave the road from time to time – to ask if it's the right road you're on. Take the child.

BASHO. If you had asked yesterday –

WANG. It's easy for you.

BASHO. – I might have listened –

WANG. You have a house! Food! Take it!

BASHO. – and made this mistake. Heaven has chosen to show me how to save you. The child alone: no.

WANG. I'll take it to the temple.

BASHO. The ordinance is against that! The priests take too many infants. The old suffer. The pediment is crumbling. When the temple is neglected, its image no longer works with the people. Then no infants are taken in! (*He points to the stool, desk, and umbrella.*) Bring these things to my carriage.

BASHO *goes out.*

WANG. How still! You face the sky. Your eyes are closed and your life is decided. (*He sits by the child and touches it.*) My father said

there were curlews once – and one called. (*He picks up the child.*)
How light. No don't smile. I must put you down. (*Still holds the child.*) You're fit and strong. You won't die.

A WOMAN *comes in, looking at* WANG. *She stops abruptly.*

WOMAN. O have I taken the wrong way? I must find the ferry.
(*She turns to go.*)

WANG. Look, a child left by the river. Often they have no limbs or they're blind. This is a fine child.

WOMAN (*looks at the child from where she stands*). Is it? I must get to the ferry.

WANG. Take it.

WOMAN. No, no.

WANG. It was left to die. Women know how to care for a child –

WOMAN. My husband is waiting.

WANG. It will die!

WOMAN. I must find the ferry –

WANG. Its hands are clutching the cover – as if it was the edge of a cliff or the side of a plate. Take it!

WOMAN (*going*). No! You!

WANG. Its eyes opened! When you spoke! Look!

WOMAN. You woke it!

WANG. Why? (*He goes with the child to the* WOMAN.) Why?

WOMAN. My husband is waiting for –

WANG. Why?

WOMAN. I'll report you to the –

WANG. Bitch! (*Hits her face.*) It could have died!

WOMAN. No. Someone would find it. You found it.

WANG. Take it!

WOMAN. No! My husband –

WANG. Your child!

WOMAN (*angrily*). You hit me! Will that make me take it? My husband hit me harder to get rid of it! It was torn from me! You think – one hit and you change the world?

WANG. It could die!

WOMAN. It was meant to die!

WANG. No!

WOMAN (*angrily*). What can I do? Our other children – it steals their food. Their stomachs are swollen. Have you heard them cry? (*She points to the child.*) This was like a disease in our house! O let me go!

WANG. No! No!

WOMAN (*sits wearily : speaks flatly, almost calmly and reasonably*). More anger . . . What is the use? You see how we live. I thought I'd jump in the river. Drown with it. But my husband – my children – I've done what I can. What more? You tell me what more there is. (*Slight pause. Still calm.*) I came back to give him water. Stupid. When I saw you holding him I was jealous. I wanted to shout 'My child!' and take him away. I was glad. You were clean and fed. The child had been lucky at last. He'll serve in a good house. (*She touches her face.*) My face is red where you hit it. I'll tell my husband I cried. (*Stands.*) I must go or he'll be suspicious.

WANG. I can't keep the child.

WOMAN. You have a dry roof! I can see that.

WANG. You don't understand.

WOMAN. And look at your coat! You have everything. Yet you ask me to take the child! I have nothing – I must even give the child away. You'll find him a corner in the house. You have a good face. You come from a good family. (*She becomes almost happy.*) My child will have a good life. Better than we could have given it. You'll teach it to be polite and bow –

WANG. This isn't the first child you've left.

WOMAN. No.

WANG. How many?

WOMAN. What's the use?

WANG. When did it start?

WOMAN. I don't think of them.

WANG. How long ago?

WOMAN. I don't know.

WANG. How did you make yourself –? Ha! it's a habit now! But the first one.

WOMAN. I didn't choose my life. These things happened to me. I don't ask anymore. I'm an animal.

WANG. You don't know what I . . . I was going away . . . Tell me . . . tell me . . . how I should live?

WOMAN (*stares at him in fear*). I didn't mean any harm.

WANG. Take this! (*He gives her* BASHO's *equipment*.) And this. All of it.

WOMAN. No! I'd –

WANG. For the child!

WOMAN. Yes. Yes. Then it's a transaction. A part of the law. I haven't left my child. I sold him. Into care. Thank you. (*She holds* BASHO's *things. Now that the child has been sold and not left to be found her self-respect comes back.*) Now – I'm a good woman and you're a good man. Tell him when he grows up to think well of people. Say I came back. Remember. I only left when I saw he was in good hands. Thank you. Goodbye, goodbye.

The WOMAN *hurries out left.* WANG *holds the child.*

WANG. Nine years – finished! I can go! Tonight! Through the door. Free. (*He stares at the child.*) What is trouble? – you don't know! Nothing changes here. I get up – I do the same things and pretend they're different. You don't even have to walk. You've been lying there for hundreds of years. I trip over you every time I come out of the door!

Why should I pick you up? Why do I hold you? You're as big as a mountain. My back's broken. I live in his house so that you have a house? Give you the things I run away from? Nine years! I planned – no, schemed, plotted, dreamt! And now you're drowning me in the river? No! No! No! No! No!

He puts the child down.

How many babies are left to die by the river? How many? For how many centuries? Left! – Rot! Eaten! Drowned! Sold! All waste! How many? Till when? All men are torn from their mother's womb: that is the law of nature. All men are torn from their mother's arms: that is the law of men! Is this all? – one little gush of sweetness and I pick up a child? Who picks up the rest? How can I hold my arms wide enough to hold them all? Feed them? Care for them? All of them? Must the whole world lie by this river like a corpse?

He snatches the child from the ground. Holds it up high to show it the river.

Look! You already have a face! Look at yourself in the river! You see your face in the mud? Look! Look! The river is a corpse that goes on devouring even when it's dead! Towns fall in! Whole generations! Their bones pile up under the bridges! You throw us in the river! Your arms are too strong! They crush me like a prison!

He puts the child down.

There's a child! (*Pointing at other imaginary children.*) There! There! There! There! You fight them off with your little hands. There! There! You little killer!

He snatches the child from the ground.

If there was a gun in your hand you'd pull it! You would kill! And you smile! Like a god playing games! As if men were your toys!
No!

As he hurls the child far out into the river he holds a corner of the white sheet in his hand and it unravels, catches the wind and falls to hang from his hand.

The world is shivering – there! Who will speak?

FIVE

Swamp.
A hand bell rung.
A group of thieves sorting loot. TIGER *and* KAKA *are thin young men.*
TIGER'*s right arm ends in a stump.* TOR-QUO *is an older and heavier*
man. SHEOUL *is a dark-haired girl.*

TIGER (*ringing*). Bell.
SHEOUL. All right.
TIGER (*ringing*). Bell. Bell.
KAKA. Mat. Torn. Not bad.
TIGER. Cap. (*Stops ringing to examine the cap.*) Fur.
SHEOUL. Fur?
TIGER. Moths. Huh! Catch! (*Throws the cap to* KAKA.)

> TOR-QUO *is upstage on the look out.*

TOR-QUO. Kaka got a knife.
KAKA. It's in. Catch. (*Throws the cap to* SHEOUL.)
TIGER (*ringing*). Bell.
SHEOUL (*picking at fur*). Fox! Lot still left. Brim's gone.
TIGER. Ding, ding. (*Rings.*) Mat. Knife. Fur cap. Good! Huh!

> (*He puts down the bell to distribute the loot.*)

SHEOUL. My cap.
TIGER. Cap – you. Tor-quo – mat.

> KAKA *rings the bell.*
> TIGER *takes bell from* KAKA.

Kaka – knife. Bell – me. (*Taps his chest with his finger.*) Musical.
KAKA (*grabs bell*). My bell! You had the whistle!
TIGER (*springs up*). Huh!
KAKA (*springs up*). Huh!

> TIGER *and* KAKA *fight violently.*

SHEOUL (*indifferently as she works at the hat*). Kill him. Break his leg. Throw him up and break his arm.

TIGER. Ha! Hoo! Grrrraaaaahhhhhhhhhh!

TOR-QUO (*to* SHEOUL). Keep it? – or make it up?

KAKA. Kill!

SHEOUL (*to* TOR-QUO. *Shrugs*). Pair of mittens? Tie on with a bit of string.

TIGER. Hah!

> TIGER *and* KAKA *stop. They are winded. They squat and face each other, breathing heavily.*

TOR-QUO. What's the food?

KAKA (*quietly*). Death.

TIGER (*quietly*). Murder.

SHEOUL (*indifferently, to* TOR-QUO). When I've finished this hat.

TIGER. Ha! Err! Hoo! Aaaghghghghghghgh!

> TIGER *and* KAKA *spring and fight.*

TOR-QUO (*reflectively*). They say you lose your appetite as you get old . . . I'm losing my hair. And my wind. And everything else . . . But I'm still hungry. It's not right . . . Look in the lining.

SHEOUL. Have. Nothing.

TOR-QUO. Found silver once.

SHEOUL. In a hat?

TOR-QUO. Boot. In the top. Dirty old working boot.

SHEOUL. Dress like tramps to trick you.

> TIGER *throws* KAKA *on his back* – KAKA *twitches senselessly on the ground.* TIGER *picks up the bell, creeps to* KAKA *with it, holds it in front of* KAKA's *face, grins slyly, waggles his stump playfully at him, pauses, grins, and finally shakes the bell – silence. He stares at the bell for a second, violently shakes it, and then looks inside – the clapper has gone.*

TIGER. Clapper! Clapper!

KAKA *groans in contentment, grasps the clapper in his hand, and rolls over to lie with it under his stomach.* TIGER *rings the bell again. It is still silent.*

TIGER (*kicking* KAKA). Clapper! Clapper! Mine!
TOR-QUO (*sudden warning*). Hup!

The others react, hide the loot and kick KAKA *to his feet.*

SHEOUL (*to* KAKA). One coming.

TIGER *lies in the ditch and pretends he has been attacked. The rest hide.*

TOR-QUO. Past the willow.
TIGER. What's he like?
TOR-QUO. Tramp.
SHEOUL. Boots?
TIGER. Kill. Kill all day today. Heeeeee.

Silence. WANG *comes on. He is dirty. His clothes are newly torn and soiled.* TIGER *groans feebly for help.*
(*Feebly.*) Help.
WANG *sits on the ground, doubles over, and cries.*

WANG. I ran through swamps, crying for seven days. I saw the rich prey on the poor. The poor prey on themselves. An old woman. She wore knitted mittens. Her hands were like a squirrel's paws – holding an empty bowl. She knelt by the pilgrims' path and said: 'Give – heaven will bless you.' What heaven would bless such pilgrims when it hadn't blessed her? Now even the marsh calls help!

WANG *hides his face and cries.* TIGER *sits up and whispers to the others.*

TIGER. Mad. (*He begins to rise in fear.*)
SHEOUL (*whisper*). Try!

TIGER *lies down again.*

TIGER (*feeble groan*). Help.

WANG (*looks up*) . . . Is someone in the swamp?

TIGER. I'm hurt. Thieves. Help me.

WANG. Alone?

TIGER. Yes. (*Tries to rise, groans, falls back.*)

WANG. Did they take much?

TIGER. Everything. But my family will pay you.

WANG. You're rich? You deserve to be robbed!

TIGER. No, no. Poor. God knows! Please. Over here. I'm drowning in the rushes!

WANG (*goes to* TIGER). Poor! – and you let yourself be robbed? That's worse! They take your money – and you offer your life! Then cry: 'Help! – pity the poor!' And someone must save you! Let someone else get blood on their hands – so you can be simple and honest and good! You deserve what you got! (*Knocks* TIGER *out with a stick.*) Learn – and next time know! Or you'll go on paying!

The other THIEVES *have crept up behind* WANG. *They throw a rope over him and bind and gag him expertly: it takes seconds.*

SHEOUL. Murderer!

TOR-QUO. Pig!

SHEOUL. Hold him!

KAKA *kneels by* TIGER *and feels his head. Roars with laughter.*

Feel that. Like an egg!

SHEOUL. It's growing.

KAKA (*laughing*). Tiger will kill you.

TOR-QUO (*sighs*). O, he'll make a mess.

KAKA (*laughs*). Tiger jabs eyes out with his stump and strangles with his hand. Hoo. (*He rocks with laughter.*) Windpipe comes out of their mouth: plop!

SHEOUL *puts out food: crackers, salt, vegetables, water.*

TOR-QUO. Food!

They eat. WANG *lies trussed on the ground.*

SHEOUL (*slaps* KAKA *to get his attention away from* WANG, *and points to* TOR-QUO *as he eats*). He'll eat it all. Hog!
KAKA (*wiping his eyes*). Squeeze – one hand.

> TIGER *groans.*
> (*Giggling.*) Kill.

SHEOUL. Save Tiger some. He'll be roaring all day.

> TIGER *groans and rocks quietly. The others eat.*

TOR-QUO (*eats*). Good.

> TIGER *groans and twists spasmodically.*

SHEOUL. Takes him time. He's worse in the mornings.
KAKA (*eating and giggling*). Kill.
TOR-QUO. Pass the salt.

> TIGER *sits up. Groans. Sees the others watching him and eating.*

TIGER. Food! Ha! (*Stands.*) Who let me sleep! Thieving bitches! (*Stops. Groans. Feels head. Remembers.*) Aaahhh! (*He sees* WANG.) Aaghghghgh! (*Runs round looking for knife.*) Knife!
KAKA. I said you'd strangle him.
TIGER. Strangle. Stab. Chop. Eat. Ha! Hoo! Eat you and spew you up in your face! (*Feels the bump.*) Head cracked. He killed me!
SHEOUL. Not cracked.
KAKA. It wouldn't show.
TIGER. Ha. Hoo. (*Reaches for food.*) Eat. Stay alive till I chop him! (*Chews frantically.*) Better! Ha!
KAKA. Undo his face. Then we can hear.

> TOR-QUO *snicks* WANG's *gag with a knife.* TIGER *breathes in* WANG's *face.*

TIGER. Haaa! Smell: Tiger. Next-time smell: You! Ha! (*He shows his stump.*) Story. How Tiger lost hand. (*The others sigh quietly.*) Ha! True! (*He sits.*) Town. I live there then. Streets. Houses. White walls. People have clean clothes. Walk in street. Children – hola! (*Imitates children's arms.*) Aahh . . . (*Sighs. All the thieves eat.*) Man. Dark eyes. In the corner shop. (*Takes more food.*) My share – you started first. (*Eats.*) Man. Bought and sold. Next – town his. Earth his. Everything goes dry. Cloth on window-sill: dry. Fields: dry. No rain: heaven forget. Ha! (*Kicks* SHEOUL *to get her attention.*) True!

SHEOUL (*eats*). True.

TIGER (*eats*). Man came. My house – sold! Walls, roof, garden, tree. Police pull me out on street. Hm. (*Chews meditatively for a moment. He speaks the next line quietly.*) Then I was quiet – before the prey. Walk to corner shop. Stand in doorway. Humble. Ask: job. Man smiles like little window high up on side of house. Beckons. So – I enter. Kow-tow. Rise. Left hand shuts his mouth. Right hand: on throat. Squeeze. Like a bag of beans. (*He holds his stump up.*) Dead. Then walk down street. Still hold. One hand: throat. Lift him up. One hand. Show. Soldiers run. Neighbours. First son. Second son. Number one wife. Number two wife. Third son. Pull. Push. Shout: Let go! I hold him up. One hand. Show. Off to court house. Judge says question: 'Have you murdered?' Hold up corpse. Show. Judge tells soldiers: 'He let's go – or chop!' Hold corpse up! High! Show! Chop! Corpse falls. Hand still on throat. Judge saw. (*Smiles at* WANG.) Ho! Tiger! (*Chews.*) Yum. Ah. Appetite come back! Ha!

WANG (*sneers*). Are you this rabble's leader?

TIGER. Ha!

WANG. There's no look out.

TIGER. Ha! (*He gets up and kicks* TOR-QUO.) Look out! Look out! Eat like pig! Look out! Ha! Fool!

TOR-QUO. I was hungry.

SHEOUL. We could have been killed.

WANG. And I haven't been searched.

TIGER (*to* KAKA). You! Search! Always! Permanent order! (*Points to* TOR-QUO.) You: kill! (*To* KAKA.) Kill! (*Waves at them all.*) Massacre!

> KAKA *and* SHEOUL *search* WANG.

SHEOUL. Nothing.

KAKA. Trousers. Jacket. Nothing.

SHEOUL. Paper.

> SHEOUL *takes* BASHO's *sheets of poems from* WANG's *pocket. The thieves stare at the papers in silence.* TIGER *walks towards them. Stops. Doesn't take the papers. They try to decipher them.*

TIGER. Tor-quo.

> TOR-QUO *comes down. He tries to decipher the papers.*

TOR-QUO. 'Flutter' . . . 'Banners.'

TIGER. Government. Official.

TOR-QUO. '. . . the arrow flies . . .'

SHEOUL (*after a silence*). Shall I undo his rope? . . . A little?

TOR-QUO. 'No man escapes his end.'

TIGER (*to* TOR-QUO). Ha!

TOR-QUO (*reads*). 'Women . . . in court.'

> *They suddenly panic.*

KAKA. A message from the emperor!

KAKA. Declaration of war!

TOR-QUO. Warrant to chop!

TIGER (*backs. Trying to control them*). We don't know! (*After a silence.*) Sir, we don't rob rich – only poor. The emperor comes on foot –

KAKA. As long as he's not in disguise.

TIGER. – and we don't hurt! We respect uniform.

TOR-QUO. And clean face.

SHEOUL. Good people. Only rob poor. To live.

TIGER. Emperor keeps people like this!

He makes a gesture with his right arm. He stares at WANG
for a response. TOR-QUO *and* KAKA *stare perplexedly at* TIGER.
SHEOUL *nudges him.* TIGER *changes the gesture to his left hand :
a thumb holding something down. The others sigh with relief.*

Emperor to look on us as helpers. If advisers tell him true.
SHEOUL (*looks at poem. Cries*). It's a pardon for poor criminals.
TIGER (*to* WANG). What does papers say?
WANG. Undo this rope.

The THIEVES *look at each other uncertainly.* TIGER *cuts the
rope.* WANG *sits up.*

Sit. (*They hesitate, then sit in a circle facing* WANG. WANG
picks up two stones.) Two stones. Hard. Dry. No moss. I strike
– thus! (*He strikes them.*) A spark! We have met – I will
tell the truth. (*The thieves glance away from him and then look
back.*) The emperor didn't send me. If the soldiers caught me
they'd cook me and eat me. I came to the swamp to find a band
of thieves. When I found them I'd join them.
TIGER (*stands swiftly, refuses*). No!
WANG. I won't join you. You're fleas under an elephant's tail.
TIGER (*rising*). Ha!
WANG. What have you got today?
TIGER. Bell. (*Rings it. It is silent.*) Good brass.
KAKA. . . . Hat.
TIGER. Fur!
SHEOUL. Knife.

TIGER *hits* KAKA, KAKA *gives him the clapper.*

TOR-QUO. Mat.
SHEOUL. Old woman's mat. Didn't she screech. Held on the end
till it tore.
TIGER (*strikes clapper on the side of the bell. It rings false – he is
holding it against his chest with his stump*). Bell. We eat. No one
catched us.

WANG. You were brave when you taught the judge to see. Now you're blinder than the judge. You have the bravery of a child: when it's angry it does anything. (*The others rise threateningly. He bows.*) Forgive my seeming rudeness. I was the servant of a great thief. He covered his floors, walls, ceilings with loot. It filled his attics and cellars. It grew in his garden. There was so much loot he built store-houses.

THE REST. Ah!

WANG. He carried it on his back. In his pockets. Other thieves guarded his loot – he paid them in loot. His hands were clean. He never raised his fist. Not even his voice. He prayed for those he sent to death. Gave money to orphans and widows. It became the meaning of ambition to follow him.

SHEOUL. That is a great thief!

WANG. I haven't told you how great yet. He had a great servant. (*He takes a bowl of water.*) This. (*He empties the bowl of water.*)

SHEOUL. Careful!

KAKA. Water!

WANG. Every year this servant raids the land. Digs up the dead to steal the coins from their mouths. Eats the fields. Strips trees. Takes men's lives. Then it's the day of judgement every day! – even when it goes back to sleep in its lair its breath stands in the fields like a white mist. What does it take: hope. What does it give: mud, to bury all things. And the people stand in their ruined fields like ghosts. They might as well be buried in them.

TOR-QUO. But the thief you worked for –

WANG. Lives on a hill. (*To* SHEOUL.) You are the poor woman. I am the thief my master. Tiger is the river. The river rises.

TIGER. Ha! Hoooooo!

WANG. I sit and smile on my hill. Where d'you run for protection?

> SHEOUL *runs away from* TIGER *to* WANG. *She brings the bundle of loot.*

I smile at the poor and weep at the flood.

SHEOUL *sits by* WANG. *He steals the bundle.*

As I weep the waters go down.

TIGER (*sits*). Ha.

WANG (*to* SHEOUL). Go home. Praise heaven.

SHEOUL *goes. She misses the bundle and comes back.*

SHEOUL. My hat!

TIGER. My chop stick!

KAKA. My knife!

TOR-QUO. My mat!

WANG. Mine. You pay for protection.

KAKA. . . . Why don't . . . the people . . . build a wall round the river? . . . Then they don't need your protection.

WANG. Tor-quo, you are my soldier! Arrest that man.

TOR-QUO (*goes to* KAKA). Sir!

WANG. And hang him.

KAKA. Why?

WANG. You stole from the woman.

KAKA. What!

WANG. Her innocence.

TIGER. Ha . . .

WANG. You see how well the landowner works. Everyman must open his mouth and drink to live. He uses the means by which men live to fill them with ignorance. They live by being condemned to death. (*Picks up a poem. As he reads the house lights come up.*) It says:

> The great thief
> Like little thieves
> Works in darkness
>
> The poor are ignorant
> They live in darkness
> What is enlightenment?
> Understanding who is the thief
> And what is the great light

Part Two

SIX

The FERRYMAN'*s house by the river. Night. The* FERRYMAN *stands in the middle of the room. His* WIFE *sits in a chair with a cover over her knees. They stare at the door and listen intently.*

WIFE (*whispering*). The path.

Silence. A knock. The FERRYMAN *looks at his* WIFE.

FERRYMAN (*whispers*). He wouldn't knock.

Another knock.

SOLDIER (*off*). Open.

The FERRYMAN *opens the door. The* FIRST SOLDIER *comes in. The* FERRYMAN *bows.* BASHO *follows the* FIRST SOLDIER *in. The* FERRYMAN *deepens his bow.*

FERRYMAN. Sir . . .

BASHO *looks round.*

FIRST SOLDIER (*points*). The mother, sir.
FERRYMAN. Does the reverend gentleman . . . ?

The FIRST SOLDIER *starts to search the room. He is casual, polite but thorough. The others pay no attention to him: they are used to soldiers searching. Everything in the room is grey except for the clothes of* BASHO *and the* SOLDIER: *they are a little brighter.*

BASHO. It's late.
FERRYMAN. My wife was unwell. It's better if she sits. If the reverend gentleman permits . . . (*The* FERRYMAN *gives his* WIFE *a bowl of water. She drinks.*)

BASHO. Last year your son's head was worth two hundred dollars. Now it's a thousand.

FIRST SOLDIER (*going behind* WIFE, *politely and routinely*.) Excuse me.

> *The* WIFE *stands, holding the cover round her legs.* BASHO *and the* FERRYMAN *pay no attention. They go on talking.*

BASHO. Did he talk of me much?

FERRYMAN. You were kind to him.

BASHO. He only talked of you when I asked. He changed.

FERRYMAN. A child grows up. They ask so many questions. Then one day they're quiet. They start to think.

BASHO. What about? Did he say?

FERRYMAN. No. He sat on the bank and stared at the water. I didn't speak to him then. I was jealous of the silence.

> *The* FIRST SOLDIER *finishes searching. He stands by the door with his hands behind his back and faces the room.*

BASHO. Were you wrong to take him from the river?

FERRYMAN (*carefully*). It was long ago.

BASHO. Would you do it again?

FERRYMAN (*carefully*). I regret what he's become. He gave us happiness when he was young.

BASHO. Where did he sleep?

FERRYMAN. That was his corner.

BASHO. I've brought your wife this.

FERRYMAN (*bows*). Sir.

BASHO. The merchant Kung-tu put his neighbour's cart up for sale. His neighbour owed for last year's seed. Then the money was thrown through the neighbour's door. Tied to a stone. But you've heard this from your passengers.

FERRYMAN. The reverend sir is right: people talk on the water. They like to tell what they think is the truth. At first I listened. I learned that my mother had been unfaithful to my father – and my breath smelt. Then I stopped listening.

BASHO. The people are the emperor's eyes and ears. The judge is his tongue. Commit to memory all that is said in your boat. Bring it to me. You may come to my house at any time. Help me to be a good judge.

FERRYMAN. The reverend sir is renowned.

BASHO. There is a small payment.

FERRYMAN. We will do our duty. As it could lead to the death of our son we should not be paid.

FIRST SOLDIER. Hh!

BASHO. Then you're not poor. Your son will cause great mischief. A few will benefit by a brief happiness. A few wrongs will be righted. Anyone can do that. But those who stand the river on end, drown the country. Do not be misled. Better to stop him now. That is hard, but true.

The FERRYMAN *bows.* BASHO *goes. The* FIRST SOLDIER *steps forward one pace. He speaks calmly and quietly, almost courteously, almost like an uncle musing over his pipe.*

FIRST SOLDIER. You people are doormats. You wait in the doorway. The street shit is rubbed in till a hole's worn in your centre. The dust collects in it like a puddle. When you're kicked out of the way, you're kicked back. Lift you up, and the dust pours out. Doormats. And soldiers worth fifty of you are dead. They didn't ask to fight for you. They don't know your names. You don't know theirs. The unknown soldiers fighting for the unknown citizens. How I rejoice when a bullet goes astray through your necks. Then I'm content. I shall watch you.

The FIRST SOLDIER *goes out. He closes the door behind him. The* FERRYMAN *and his* WIFE *are alone. For a moment they talk in artificially high voices.*

WIFE. A whole jar.

FERRYMAN. Best honey.

WIFE. You must find out all you can to help the judge.

FERRYMAN. Yes.

The FERRYMAN *goes to the door, listens, turns back to his* WIFE. *She stares at him in fear.*

(*Whispering urgently.*) He wouldn't come – with the soldiers outside.

WIFE. We shouldn't have told him.

FERRYMAN. He must know.

WIFE. It's better to keep it to ourselves . . .

FERRYMAN. Perhaps it's too dangerous to come.

WIFE. There are old grandmothers who walk like girls. If I'd eaten better and kept warm in the wet winters I'd still look young. I went without food till I was so weak I had to hold on to things to stand. The skin shrivelled on my hands. I was grey so soon. He got bigger and stronger. I heard him running on the bank. Shouting. What luck! – to give my life and see him grow. Then I became his mother – I died in this slow childbirth. He fed me later. But the damage was done. Inside. That couldn't be put… (*Remembering* WANG *as a child has made her quietly happy. Now her strength goes again. Her voice becomes flat and mechanical.*) I wanted to live and see him come home from work, hold the arms of my chair – so there was a little jolt – and kiss me. I wanted to teach his wife and scold her a little. Mothers-in-law shouldn't be too easy. I learned from my mother-in-law. She'd be a good girl. One day I'd hold their child. It was a dream. Well.

FERRYMAN. He was a good son.

WIFE. Even that man was fond of him in his way.

FERRYMAN. Basho? – When a guttering candle goes out it stinks.

A hand has come through a loose paper window-pane. It lifts the pane cautiously : outside someone is looking in. The FERRYMAN *points to warn his* WIFE. *He sits. The door opens.* WANG *and* TIGER *come in.*

FERRYMAN. Soldiers! –

WANG. They've gone!

FERRYMAN. Is it safe?

WANG. If we're quick. I've got a look-out. (*He embraces the* WIFE.) Good. Good. Yes. (*Embraces the* FERRYMAN.) Father. Good. Is the boat all right?

FERRYMAN. Yes. I think it –

WIFE. You came. You came.

FERRYMAN. I said he would.

WANG. We need your help.

FERRYMAN. Our help?

WANG. You know what a rifle is? We're arming the villages.

FERRYMAN (*blankly*). A rifle? You have rifles?

WANG. From a merchant. A westerner. A lot. In the swamp. You look surprised! Yes – isn't it good! What did you think we did with our money?

TIGER. Ha! Women! Concubines! Wine!

WANG. We loot the big houses. Raid convoys. Kidnap. Blackmail. Take hostages. Now we're rich we don't count our money in cash. We say: 'How many rifles are we worth?'

FERRYMAN (*blank*). Rifles?

WANG. Yes! For the villages!

FERRYMAN (*confused*). Clothes – food – bedding – medicine. But rifles?

WANG. To fight the landowner. We can take over the villages with rifles.

FERRMAN (*turns in confusion to his* WIFE). He's talking of rifles –

WANG. To take to the villages. In your boat.

His WIFE *stands in front of her chair. The cover is round her legs.*

Then everything follows: Food, clothes, bedding, medicine – and more! Understanding, knowledge –

FERRYMAN. You take from the landowner. Good. We get a half-sack of rice! But understanding, knowledge –

WANG. That is a good question, but –

FERRYMAN (*cutting in angrily*). Will heaven like you so much it works miracles for you?

WANG. We'll build the river banks –

FERRYMAN (*shaking his head*). I don't understand!

WANG. We're poor because there's little to go round. Why? Because the river floods. Why? The mouth is silted. The banks are down. There's no cut-off channel for the spring water –

FERRYMAN (*trying to think*). Why doesn't the landowner build banks? Rifles? Rifles?

WANG. Why should the landowner build banks? He's rich. Why? Because we're poor. Why are we poor? Because we're ignorant. Why ignorant? Because the bank breaks and takes away all we have. We're like cattle who live in the mud. Even when the sun shines the people who live on the bank are afraid. They shake and their faces are white. Fear, flies, disease, famine. The landowner needs to do one thing. Only one. Keep us in ignorance. The river does that for him. So take the river and make it ours! That's why rifles are food and clothes and knowledge!

TIGER (*to* WIFE). Rifles! In swamp! Ha!

WANG. You must take them across the river.

FERRYMAN. Did you get my message?

WANG. Yes.

FERRYMAN. Your mother –

WANG. Yes. The message came.

WIFE. The midwife says – a growth (*touches herself*) – I have only a little more time.

WANG. Is the pain . . . ?

WIFE (*after a slight pause; shakes head*). No.

> TIGER *gives a slight grunt.* WANG *turns to the* FERRYMAN.

WANG. You'll help?

FERRYMAN. The soldiers watch us.

WANG. They watch everyone. You're called a saint. They'll trust you more than the rest.

FERRYMAN. Make a boat.

WANG. A new boat would be stopped. Especially at night. Hide the rifles under the boards. We hid the fish.

TIGER (*to the* FERRYMAN). See! We make so much trouble – enemy brings many soldiers – enemy now strong – *we* get strong – or chop! (*To* WIFE.) See! Too late to go back! (*Points to* WANG.) Him – me – everyone: chop! (*To* FERRYMAN.) Ha?

FERRYMAN. No.

WANG. Then you're an enemy.

FERRYMAN. No.

WANG. Yes! If you don't help now, you'll make other mistakes! Listen to their arguments too long. Hesitate. Be patient at the wrong time. One day people like you will take us to be shot!

FERRYMAN. No. I want to do what is good. Wang – help the poor. Give them . . . but if I was caught (*He looks at his* WIFE.) . . . she . . .

WANG. I know.

TIGER (*picks up the jar, suddenly suspicious*). Honey!

FERRYMAN. Basho. My wife. He told me to spy. A sort of bribe.

WANG. Even better! (*To* TIGER.) We'll give him information to pass on. Nothing to cause real damage. (*To the* FERRYMAN.) He'll trust you and your boat won't be stopped. (*Slight silence.*) You picked me up and took me home. A good man! The good ferryman! The saint who lives by the river! Do the birds sing when you come through your door? It's not easy to do good. You pick up one child. What about the tenth child? Or the hundredth child? You leave them to rot! Drown them with your holy hands.

The WIFE *sits.*

FERRYMAN. It was hard to bring you up to –

WANG. You saints who crucify the world so that you can be good! You keep us in dirt and ignorance! Force us into the mud with your dirty morality! You are the scourge of the –. No, no, I must understand. I must be patient. I'm sorry. – Father. (*He takes the* FERRYMAN *aside.*) She'll die *soon* – your message said–

FERRYMAN. Wang!

WANG. It's true!

FERRYMAN (*fiercely, quietly angry*). But not dragged out by her hair – thrown into a ring of soldiers with knives. I love her!

WANG. But you took her life!

FERRYMAN. No!

WANG. When you took me from the river! You starved her – crippled her – she's dying now because you took –

FERRYMAN. I love her!

WANG. And you killed her!

FERRYMAN. Aieeeeeeeeee!

WANG. O we are little men! We love – and think that changes the world! I have done nothing that you have not done before!

FERRYMAN. Aieeee!

A moment's silence.

WIFE. Yes, I will die. But you mustn't speak to your father like that. The night he brought you home I shut the door. He sat with you in the boat. I said: 'Good, let him be cold.' He put up the little canvas awning. It flapped in the wind. You started to cry so he cried too. Sat in the boat and cried with you. You were a greedy child. Always after more. We gave it – when we could. You are right, that's why I've lived like a cripple and can't fight this sickness. And now – strange – you come over the river – hiding for your life – and ask for more – not with a gun – but something stronger – even stronger – as you've shown. Father, do what he wants.

FERRYMAN. Yes. If you'd drowned in the river someone else would have been asked the same question. I'll take the rifles. I've loved and hated. The river kept me alive and almost killed me. Now it will carry the rifles. I shall be careful. Your mother will be safe.

WANG. So we go on. The rifles will come in threes. If anything goes wrong we won't lose many. Leave them out in the boat. Come in the house. Don't look. They'll be taken away. We'll warn you each time we're coming. It'll be finished in six weeks.

WIFE (*to* WANG). Here. Let me hold you. (*She holds* WANG *against her, strokes him and makes soothing noises as if he were a child.*) There. There. My child.

TIGER *talks excitedly to the* FERRYMAN *at one side.*

TIGER. Once a judge said: 'Execute.' (*Points at himself.*) Chop! I escape? How?

FERRYMAN (*blankly*). What?

TIGER. Story! True. Listen. Soldiers take me to town. More people to see chop! Walk all day. Hot. Dust. Girls stare. Children. (*Waves arms like a child.*)

WIFE (*nursing* WANG). There. There. It will be all right. (*She cries quietly as she rocks him.*)

WANG. Mother.

TIGER. Riot in town! Barracks upside down! Drink on sale. Soldiers give me to jailer. True! (*Nudges the* FERRYMAN.)

FERRYMAN (*half listening*). Yes.

WIFE (*nursing* WANG *against her breast. Rocking and crying quietly*). This is our last time. Thank you. Thank you.

WANG. Thank you.

TIGER. Jailer takes me to cell. Iron chain on wall. Ring. Bolt. I whimper like christian. Clasp hands under shawl – hold out to pray – so! Jailer knows nothing. Heaven smiles. Jailer puts ring round right arm. Click. Goes out. Wait. Soldiers drunk. Doors open. Night. Slip arm through ring: hup! Walk home.

FERRYMAN. Home?

TIGER (*giggles*). Ha! They say: 'Tiger has one hand but fights with ten.'

WANG *leaves the* WIFE.

WANG. We must go.

TIGER. God has ten hands. Each side. Good for miracles. But never escape.

WANG (*angrily to* TIGER). Quickly.

WANG *goes out.*

TIGER. Life good. Wise say: 'Give hand in friendship.' Tiger raise stump: Great Friend!

> TIGER *hurries off after him.*

WIFE. Help me to lie down.

SEVEN

Roadside between the villages. The WOMAN, *from Scene Four, sits on the ground with her* HUSBAND. *She wears a stone cangue closed with a bolt. The* SECOND SOLDIER *sits on guard at the back. Down left, the* FIRST WATER SELLER. *He has a water can, cups, a towel and a picture of snow falling on a mountain. The* SECOND SOLDIER *sits on guard at the back.*

FIRST WATER SELLER. No one will buy anything! If you'd done one good deed – someone would come! The judge was right! You're an evil woman!

> *The* WOMAN *groans to quieten the* WATER SELLER.

I've sat here an hour! Not one cup!

HUSBAND. Is it still morning?

FIRST WATER SELLER. Soldier, you're thirsty.

SECOND SOLDIER. Your wife pisses in it to make it go further.

> *The* FIRST WATER SELLER *doesn't bother to defend himself. The* SECOND WATER SELLER *comes on. He carries a picture of a temple.*

FIRST WATER SELLER. Hey! Clear off!

SECOND WATER SELLER. The road's wide enough for two.

FIRST WATER SELLER. I got them first!

SECOND WATER SELLER (*unloading his equipment*). Pure water!

FIRST WATER SELLER. Clear off! I was here when you were still snoring on top of your woman.

SECOND WATER SELLER. Pure water! Water from the temple well!

FIRST WATER SELLER (*to* SECOND SOLDIER). Arrest him! Hey! Send him off!

SECOND SOLDIER. No law against two.

FIRST WATER SELLER. I was here first!

SECOND SOLDIER. You won't be here last!

FIRST WATER SELLER. It's not justice! He's taking my livelihood! Get out! – or I'll chuck your water out!

SECOND WATER SELLER. Soldier, this tradesman is threatening a disturbance. (*Points to the* WOMAN *and her* HUSBAND.) I've got witnesses.

FIRST WATER SELLER. I'll break your cups! They can witness that!

SECOND SOLDIER. I'll break your heads!

FIRST WATER SELLER. You won't sell water. You'll float in it.

SECOND SOLDIER. A war would be better than rotting here. You're all thieves. I'd hang the lot. I was in a garrison town. Coloured lights in the evenings. The whorehouses had orchestras. Fried rice on the stalls. We had the girls under the trees by the park in the evenings. Then they dragged us here. And you expect us to feel sorry you're –

The WATER SELLERS *see something off stage. They start to call their wares.*

FIRST WATER SELLER.
Water! Sparkling water!
The moon shone on the snow
As it fell on the muses' mountain
I melted the snow at dawn
Sparkling water!
Who drinks speaks truth!

SECOND WATER SELLER.
Water! Pure water!
From the temple well
Of the goddess of truth
I drew it
From the dark cool well
Who drinks sees truth!

The WATER SELLERS *bang their cups on their cans.* TIGER and
WANG *come on left. They are disguised as priests.*

SECOND WATER SELLER (*aside*   FIRST WATER SELLER (*groans*).
to the WOMAN, *pointing to her*   Ugh, priests! (*Aside to the*
HUSBAND, *who is asleep*). Get   WOMAN.) Make the best of
grandad going! If it's a good   it. Put on a good show. I'll
sale it'll be worth your while!   give you two cups.

The WOMAN *shakes her husband awake.*

HUSBAND. Water . . . water . . . water . . .

FIRST WATER SELLER. The   SECOND WATER SELLER. Holy
woman's suffered all her life.   fathers, the woman has this
A terrible home! They beat   sick husband. Their sons are
her not the mule! The whole   ungrateful. They ran away as
village pities her! 'Poor woman,'   soon as they could. Thirst
they say, 'never out of trouble.'   has tormented her three
                                   days. Buy her a little water!

WOMAN (*crying*). The court said I was guilty . . . It was only a
crime on earth . . . In heaven the gods would have blessed
me . . . I stole for my husband.

SECOND SOLDIER. Strangers?

WANG. Pilgrim priests who travel from temple to temple. Our
footprints are in the dust of a hundred shrines.

FIRST WATER SELLER. Don't buy his grandmother's pee holy
fathers! It's wrong to sell that even to tax collectors! But to holy
fathers – it's sacrilege!

SECOND WATER SELLER. Don't listen to that trafficker in dogs'
urine. Taste how fresh my water is! Tears of pity!

The WOMAN *whimpers.*

WANG. We have no money.

FIRST WATER SELLER. Then don't come begging here!

SECOND WATER SELLER. Clear off! Layabouts! We were here
before you!

The WATER SELLERS *go back to their pitches.* WANG *and* TIGER *come downstage.*

WANG (*to* TIGER). Ask her why she's punished.

TIGER. The meeting –

WANG. Ask her!

TIGER (*goes to the* WOMAN). Why are you punished?

WOMAN. Stealing.

HUSBAND. Cabbage leaves.

WOMAN. He needed broth.

SECOND SOLDIER. That's what she was *caught* for! Don't pity them. You think they live in ruins? They've all got so much loot under the floor their houses are lopsided.

TIGER *goes back to* WANG.

WOMAN (*to the* SECOND SOLDIER). Soldier, the stone is heavy. Can my husband help me?

SECOND SOLDIER (*shrugs*). Has he got the strength?

The HUSBAND *tries to take some of the weight of the cangue.* TIGER *and* WANG *are downstage.*

WOMAN. The weight off my neck. Yes.

TIGER. The village elders are waiting –

WANG. Sit. (*He pulls* TIGER *down. They sit in the lotus position.*)

TIGER. Ah – kill the soldier and break the stone? Let me get close. He won't suspect priests.

WANG. No!

TIGER. Her husband's tears run down the stone. It's quiet outside the village. One soldier. (*He gestures with his stump.*) My hand itches.

WANG. No.

TIGER. People who did this – they made your parents leave you by the river. Ha! Show them change coming! Tonight their feather pillows like stones. (*Gestures with his stump.*) When this hand itches: means good deed!

WANG. I know the woman. I'd help her before all others. I sit
   here calmly. I bite the inside of my lip to stop shouting out. Look,
   there is blood inside my mouth –

TIGER. And my hand itches!

WANG. Too soon.

TIGER. Then buy her water!

WANG. Worse!

TIGER. Hard!

WANG (*there is a sudden fall of blood from* WANG's *mouth. As he
   talks it runs down his chin*). No. The ox bears the yoke. Break
   the yoke. Another yoke is put on its neck. The farmer has fifty
   yokes in his store. Stop being an ox. What is the use of breaking
   a window when it has iron bars? The landowner still controls.
   When he needs soldiers he sends – and they come. So people
   fear him. If we're kind to the women – he must be crueller to
   the people. So they say: 'She deserves to be punished.' They act
   out of fear. That is their morality. The only morality they can
   have. Learn it: the government makes not only laws, but
   a morality, a way of life, what people are in their very nature.
   We have not yet earned the right to be kind. I say it with blood
   in my mouth. When the landowner is no longer feared then
   our kindness will move mountains. That is our morality, Tiger.
   Today we should look on kindness with suspicion. Here only
   the evil can afford to do good.

   KUNG-TU *comes on.*

FIRST WATER SELLER.   SECOND WATER SELLER.
   Water! Sparkling water!   Water! Pure water!
   The moon shone on the snow   From the temple well
   That fell on –   Of the –

   The WATER SELLERS *break off. They smile in anticipation –
   knowing what will happen.*

FIRST WATER SELLER. Kung-tu.

SECOND WATER SELLER. His nephew owned the cabbage leaves. Be merciful Kung-tu!

FIRST WATER SELLER. Earn remission in heaven!

SECOND WATER SELLER. Don't teach him about earning.

FIRST WATER SELLER. I wouldn't try to cheat Kung-Tu. How could I get mountain water at a sellable price? It's from a clean stretch of the river. I carried it on my back for an hour. It would taste like mountain water to her, so I haven't lied.

SECOND WATER SELLER. That's water from down-river. Mine is up-river water! And cheap at the –

KUNG-TU. Shut up. (*To* WOMAN.) You did wrong.

WOMAN. My husband's ill. Our children left home. They can't beg for us *and* themselves.

KUNG-TU. Did you do wrong?

TIGER (*to* WANG). We must go.

WANG. Watch. Learn.

HUSBAND. She saw from my face I was hungry. If I'd hidden my face from my wife all would have been well. I'm to blame.

The RICE CRACKER MAN *comes in.*

RICE CRACKER MAN. Rice crackers!
    The rice crackers lay on the table
    To cool from the oven
    The moon passing over the table
    Stopped at the crackers an hour
    To taste them: food for the gods!

FIRST WATER SELLER. Get out! He's buying water!

SECOND WATER SELLER. Mouse bait!

RICE CRACKER MAN (*aside to the* WATER SELLERS). They're salty today.

FIRST WATER SELLER. O these are the famous Moon Rice Crackers.

SECOND WATER SELLER. The soldier should try this local delicacy.

SECOND SOLDIER. A starving dog wouldn't howl for them.

KUNG-TU. Two rice crackers. Two cups of water. One from the temple of truth. One from the muses' mountain.

FIRST WATER SELLER. Everyone respects Kung-tu.

SECOND WATER SELLER. His own worst enemy.

RICE CRACKER MAN. They'll name a march after him one day!

The WATER SELLERS *pour two cups of water. The* RICE CRACKER MAN *puts two rice crackers on the ground.*

TIGER (*to* WANG). The meeting!

WANG. Wait. Learn!

TIGER. It's dangerous here!

KUNG-TU. Fathers, my heart is full of a natural pity. It brims! Shall I give in? Or be stern for the good of the community?

WANG. We're in meditation. Lost in wonder. Deep in thought.

KUNG-TU. I've never studied theology. So I'll have to give in. A man without feelings is a stone.

KUNG-TU *hands the water and crackers to the* WOMAN *and her* HUSBAND. *They eat and drink.*

WOMAN. Thank you. Thank you.

HUSBAND. Thank you.

KUNG-TU. Look, the woman's lips can't help smiling now they're wet. His hand is shaking for joy.

THIRD SOLDIER *comes on.*

THIRD SOLDIER. Back to barracks.

SECOND SOLDIER. Another action? I didn't get the regulation sleep last night.

THIRD SOLDIER. The landowner's leaving.

KUNG-TU. Leaving?

THIRD SOLDIER (*raising his voice for all of them to hear*). For a few weeks. To visit the capital. (*To the* SECOND SOLDIER.) He wanted an escort. We're on barrack duty.

SECOND SOLDIER. Better than this.

THIRD SOLDIER (*to the* WOMAN). Squat in the village.

FIRST WATER SELLER. Water!

THIRD SOLDIER. I wouldn't wash a dead rat's foreskin in that.

The SOLDIERS *go.*

KUNG-TU (*panicking*). The landowner leaving. That's why the carts weren't sent out to the fields this morning. He's taking all his stuff. A short visit? (*Shrugs. Tries to reassure himself.*) We've got the soldiers. They're our bridge tower wall in one! . . . When this gets out the shop will be busy. People panic – they're silly enough – and hoard food. (*Uneasily.*) A short visit? I must get back . . . (*Gets a grip on himself.*) And at times like these supplies don't get through.

KUNG-TU *hurries out left.*

WANG. Break the cangue.

TIGER. Now?

WANG. Yes.

TIGER. Ha! Why?

WANG. The landowner's run. We worked underground at the foundations. No one saw. But the walls shook. Now – suddenly – a brick falls from the top! The first sign of weakness. The people see it – a sign of our strength! The wall cracks! Now pull it down!

TIGER *and* WANG *run to the* WOMAN. *The* WATER SELLERS *and the* RICE CRACKER MAN *stop packing their equipment.*

WOMAN. Fathers!

TIGER *and* WANG *kneel by the* WOMAN.

TIGER. Ha!

WOMAN. What is –? Help!

TIGER *takes out his gun.* WANG *takes out an iron cosh. He gently pushes the* WOMAN *over till the cangue rests on the ground.*

WOMAN (*screams*). Help!

TIGER. Quiet! Or –! (*Threatens her* HUSBAND *with his gun.*)

WANG (*struggling with the* WOMAN). Still! We've come to help!

HUSBAND (*bewildered*). Help . . . ?

FIRST WATER SELLER. What is –?

SECOND WATER SELLER. Help!

> TIGER *covers everyone with his gun.*

RICE CRACKER MAN (*sees* TIGER's *stump and recognizes him*). Look! – the stump!

TIGER. Quick!

> WANG *hits the stone with the hammer. Blows ring out. The* WOMAN *screams.*

WOMAN (*struggling*). No, no, no. Don't kill me.

HUSBAND. Help us . . .

TIGER. Shut up!

WANG. Like iron.

TIGER. Towels! (*He runs to the* WATER SELLERS, *takes their towels, throws them to* WANG.) Quick!

WOMAN (*while* TIGER *gets the towels*). Please. No. (*She is paralysed with fear.*) Don't kill me. (*To the* WATER SELLERS *and* RICE CRACKER MAN.) I didn't ask. You saw. They forced me –

HUSBAND (*terrified*). Please. The soldiers.

> WANG *muffles the stone with the towels and begins to hit it again.*

WANG (*quiet, intense*). Now see – who is the stone – on the people's neck! And who is the stone breaker.

> *The stone falls apart. The* WOMAN *sits up. She doesn't dare to move her neck or even look down. She stares straight ahead.*

SECOND WATER SELLER. Don't shoot.

FIRST WATER SELLER. We didn't see it.

RICE CRACKER MAN. We'd gone.

TIGER (*quietly*). Haghghghgh!

TIGER *and* WANG *go out right.*

WOMAN (*in tears*). Tell the soldiers you saw. I tried to stop it.
HUSBAND (*in tears*). We tried. I'm always too weak.

The WATER SELLERS, *the* RICE CRACKER MAN, *the* WOMAN *and her* HUSBAND *stare at the pieces of stone. The* WATER SELLERS *hurriedly snatch up their towels and hide them.*

FIRST WATER SELLER. What shall we do?
RICE CRACKER MAN. If only the soldiers hadn't seen us!
FIRST WATER SELLER. Say we left.
SECOND WATER SELLER. No – run them to barracks!
RICE CRACKER MAN. No! No! Fool!
SECOND WATER SELLER. Fool? Why?
FIRST WATER SELLER (*gestures off after* WANG *and* TIGER). They saw us!

Silence. They realize their situation.

SECOND WATER SELLER (*dull fear*). O god we're between two tigers. My father said: 'Never between two tigers.

The WOMAN *whimpers quietly as she feels her neck. They all talk in whispers.*

FIRST WATER SELLER. Give them some water.
SECOND WATER SELLER. Give . . . ?
FIRST WATER SELLER. Everything's changed.
RICE CRACKER MAN. And they need water.
SECOND WATER SELLER (*puzzled, unsure*). Give them . . . ?

They still talk in whispers.

FIRST WATER SELLER. Yes.
RICE CRACKER MAN. Yes.

They all stare at one another in amazement. They hardly believe what they're doing.

SECOND WATER SELLER (*observing himself in amazement, watching the running water as if it were the first time he had seen it, handling the water can as if it had just dropped from space*). . . . I pour the water . . .

FIRST WATER SELLER (*staring at his own hand as it moves; almost whispering*). I take the cup and . . .

> The FIRST WATER SELLER *hands the cup to the* WOMAN. *He stares at his hand holding the cup of water.*

RICE CRACKER MAN. Drink.

> *They watch in silent amazement as the* WOMAN *drinks half the water and gives the rest to her* HUSBAND. *She watches the* WATER SELLERS *as her* HUSBAND *drinks.*

FIRST WATER SELLER (*quietly, unsure, amazed, puzzled, calm, without boasting*). We gave her the water to drink.

> *They straighten up. The* WOMAN *and her* HUSBAND *stand. Silence. They become tense and stare anxiously.*

Now . . .

HUSBAND. The soldiers . . .

RICE CRACKER MAN. *Hide!*

FIRST WATER SELLER. And show the stones in the villages.

> *They pick up the stones and hurry out left.*

EIGHT
(a)

FERRYMAN'*s house. Night.*
BASHO *and the* FIRST SOLDIER *have just come in.*
The FERRYMAN *rises from his bow.*
His WIFE *stares from the chair.*

FERRYMAN. Sir.

BASHO. You did not come to see me.

FERRYMAN. I had nothing to tell.

BASHO. No one has used your ferry?

FERRYMAN. They were silent.

BASHO. When did you see your son?

FERRYMAN. Not since he left the service of the reverend –

FIRST SOLDIER (*calm disgust*). Tch.

FERRYMAN. The soldier accuses me? I humbly beg to be believed –

The FIRST SOLDIER *makes a short sound of anger and disgust.*

BASHO. You had the chance to clear yourself. You might have acted from fear. But you speak this to my face. I see how your son was taught.

The FIRST SOLDIER *goes to the door, opens it, briefly looks out, and turns back to the room, leaving the door open.*

You carry rifles over the river.

FERRYMAN (*bows slightly, shaking his head, not looking at the open door*). People denounce their neighbours out of fear. Or spite.

The SECOND *and* THIRD SOLDIERS *come through the open door. They support* TIGER *between them – though he can walk unaided. His hair and face are covered with several patchy layers of dry, faded blood. The upper part of his body is knotted in a sheet.*

BASHO. You meet your son at night. You take the rifles over the water in the bottom of your boat. Then they're taken into the villages. You meet him again tonight. (*To the* FIRST SOLDIER.) I'll be by the window.

BASHO *goes out. The* FIRST SOLDIER *speaks and acts without salacious violence. He is calm, almost courteous. The* SOLDIERS *are used to their work and too bored with it to enjoy it. Really they act out of fear – amateur mountain climbers : a show of calm, hollow inside.*

FIRST SOLDIER. Once Tiger roared. The roaring got on our nerves. We're only human. We like working conditions to be as good as circumstances allow. After all, a prison's not a zoo. Now Tiger does farmyard imitations. He's lost his tongue. (*Points to the* THIRD SOLDIER.) He's a real tearaway. (*To* TIGER.) Do chicken.

> TIGER *imitates a chicken: a residual noise in the back of his throat.*

Chicken with twisted neck. Now sheep.

> TIGER *makes the same sound.*

Good. Now the big one. Do pig.

> TIGER *makes the same sound.*

(*Reasonably.*) He's not trying. Someone show him.

> *The* THIRD SOLDIER *lifts his foot from the ground and lowers it.* TIGER *goes down on all fours. The* WIFE *quietly covers her head with the cover.*

That's the right posture for well brought up pig. Tiger told a great story – how he lost his hand. A lie, of course. Lost it for pick-pocketing. No more stories. Pity. (*Imitation.*) 'Tiger has true story tell now. How Tiger lost other hand.' (*Points to the* THIRD SOLDIER.) He collects memos of the departed. It was like chopping branches off a tree. I thought he'd get to the roots.

THIRD SOLDIER (*laughs flatly at the bad joke.*)

FIRST SOLDIER. As for the present: you take out the boat. Meet the enemy. We lie in the bottom. I look round this room to find something valuable enough to break. Nothing's of value to me. But standards change from the point of view.

FERRYMAN. I wouldn't –

FIRST SOLDIER. You will. That's how it will always be. That's why I'm here. Answering. Not asking for questions.

The FIRST SOLDIER *nods. The* SECOND SOLDIER *goes to window and raps on the paper pane.*

I can't promise you your life. That's out. No pardons. (*Shakes head.*) Not that it's up to me. Or the judge. The government's said it. But there's no need for your wife to be killed. She's senile enough not to know what you were up to. When my word's given it's kept.

BASHO *comes in.*

BASHO. We'll wait.
FERRYMAN (*to the* FIRST SOLDIER, *points to* TIGER). Some water . . . ?
FIRST SOLDIER. Why bother? Too late.

The FERRYMAN *holds a cup of water for* TIGER *to drink.* TIGER *drinks messily and greedily.*

BASHO (*suddenly very angry*). I said wait! In quiet!
FIRST SOLDIER (*to the other* SOLDIERS). Outside.

The THIRD SOLDIER *takes the bowl from* TIGER's *mouth. The* SECOND *and* THIRD SOLDIERS *take* TIGER *out through the door. The* FIRST SOLDIER *closes it behind them. The* FERRYMAN *still holds the bowl.*

Sorry, sir. Not long. Dark three hours.
BASHO. Yes.
FERRYMAN. The judge is wise. I'm old and foolish. My love for our son made me a traitor. My wife wasn't told. Now all this is known I'm at peace. I don't meet him tonight. (*Points after* TIGER.) He said what you made him. Let me live here under the soldiers' watch till my son sends a message. Then I'll make amends.
BASHO (*to the* FIRST SOLDIER). The staff meeting may last longer now. Your second in command can take charge of the search.

FIRST SOLDIER. Sir.

BASHO. Tell him not to pick the area till an hour before-hand.

> *The* TWO SOLDIERS *come back, shut the door behind them and wait in the background.*

THIRD SOLDIER. Nothing outside yet.

SECOND SOLDIER. A bit of moon.

FERRYMAN (*simply and calmly, as if he no longer had to struggle with his thoughts but knew what to say. He holds the water in front of him. Close to his chest*). Why are our lives wasted? We have minds to see how we suffer. Why don't we use them to change the world? A god would wipe us off the board with a cloud: a mistake. But as there is only ourselves shouldn't we change our lives so that we don't suffer? Or at least suffer only in changing them? (*Noiselessly, carefully he puts down the bowl.*)

> *The ferry bell in the distance: one stroke.*

FIRST SOLDIER. Outside.

FERRYMAN. I'll light the lamp.

FIRST SOLDIER (*bored and angry*). Outside.

> *The* FERRYMAN, BASHO *and the* FIRST *and* THIRD SOLDIERS *go out. The* SECOND SOLDIER *and the* WIFE *are left. The* SECOND SOLDIER *pokes out one of the window panes with his fist. He peers through the hole for a moment. He turns and goes to the* WIFE.

SECOND SOLDIER. I'll tie your mouth. Then you don't need to shout. That won't help.

> *The* SECOND SOLDIER *gags the* WIFE.

(b)

This scene is played on the front of the stage. The SECOND SOLDIER *and the* WIFE *remain motionless in the* FERRYMAN'*s house.*

Far bank of the river, by the bell pole. Dark. WANG, SHEOUL *and* PU-TOI *wait. They are armed with rifles.*

PU-TOI. Listen!
WANG. He's started!
SHEOUL. I wish the moon would go.
WANG. It will.

    They listen in silence.

We wait by the river. My mother came here. And left me. Do you call her a criminal? Perhaps in a month she was dead in the gutter. Perhaps she reached up out of the gutter to put me here. Now we'll help those like her.

The young set out from this river. The old return to die. Merchants cross day after day till their lives are as soiled and faceless as old money. Orders are sent to buy or sell or accuse. Thieves plot while they wait on this worn-out landing. Soldiers with blood down to their undercloths. Monks without the child's right to innocence, with faces like snakes or pampered old women. They all came here, waited, stepped into the boat and trusted their lives to the dark river that crosses their path even as they pass over on it.

This time we wait with rifles – and the ferryman comes to meet us.
SHEOUL. I'll fetch the rifles.
WANG. When he's nearer. (*To* PU-TOI.) Keep watch up the bank.

    PU-TOI *moves off in the dark.*

Tie this to a rifle.
SHEOUL. What?
WANG. A note for my mother.

    SHEOUL *takes the note into the bush.*

(*Whispering to* SHEOUL.) There! In the dark against the horizon. – The rifles!

SHEOUL brings three rifles, bound in sacking to the landing place.

In the bushes. See it all goes well.

Splash. The sound of the ferry pole falling in the water.

SHEOUL. What –?
WANG. The guns!

SHEOUL and WANG run from the bushes, she takes the rifles out left, WANG covers her with his rifle, PU-TOI runs in.

PU-TOI. What –?
WANG. *The pole! He dropped it!*
PU-TOI. The guns!
WANG. Here!

WANG and PU-TOI run out after SHEOUL. Subdued whispers from the water.

FIRST SOLDIER. . . . there . . .
FERRYMAN. . . . got . . .

Slight pause. The FERRYMAN walks out of the darkness on to the landing place. Calls softly.

Wang . . . The boat . . .

Turns to the SOLDIERS hidden in the dark, as if for instructions.

I . . . ?

Suddenly the SOLDIERS jump on to the land. They run frantically up and down the bank searching.

THIRD SOLDIER. No one.
FIRST SOLDIER. No sign?
THIRD SOLDIER. Nothing.

The FIRST SOLDIER fumbles to light a lamp. He holds it over their heads.

The landing place is worn flat. Nothing to tell from this.

FIRST SOLDIER. Pig. How did he get tipped off?

THIRD SOLDIER. Or Tiger lied.

FIRST SOLDIER. Pig it. We've killed him. (*To the* FERRYMAN.) Get in.

They all vanish in the darkness in the direction of the boat.

(c)

FERRYMAN'*s hut.* SECOND SOLDIER, *the* WIFE *and* BASHO. BASHO *is nervous.*

SECOND SOLDIER (*looking through the hole in the window*). Them sir.

The SECOND SOLDIER *knocks out the rest of the window with his rifle butt – there is no need to hide their presence any more. The frame falls out neatly, leaving a black hole shaped like a TV screen.*

BASHO. Alone? There was no shouting . . .

SECOND SOLDIER (*peering out*). Too dark to . . .

BASHO. Undo her mouth.

The SECOND SOLDIER *crosses to the* WIFE *to unfasten her gag. Sound of the boat tapping the wooden landing place and the* FIRST SOLDIER *saying 'Hup!' The* SECOND SOLDIER *returns to the window. The* WIFE *is still gagged.*

SECOND SOLDIER (*peering out*). They're back, sir.

BASHO. Who's with them?

SECOND SOLDIER (*peering out*). It's dark . . .

Slight pause. The FIRST SOLDIER *appears head and shoulders in the open window.*

FIRST SOLDIER (*in the window*). No one, sir. (*Pause.* BASHO *doesn't answer.*) Sir.

BASHO. Tell me what happened.

FIRST SOLDIER. We crossed the river. He called as we said. We kept quiet. Even when he dropped the pole.

BASHO. He dropped the pole in the water?

FIRST SOLDIER. Sir.

BASHO. Is he there?

FIRST SOLDIER. Sir.

> BASHO *raises his voice for the* FERRYMAN *to hear. The* FERRY-MAN *isn't seen. The head and shoulders of the* FIRST SOLDIER *stay in the window as he turns to look off, left, to the* FERRYMAN.

BASHO. A haiku is made of seventeen syllables in three lines in the order of five, seven and five. These lines are short and clean – like the strokes of a pole driving a boat through the water. You've ferried your boat long enough to know about haiku. You'll understand what I say next. In haiku the lines come to the master complete. Each line enters the head the moment the line before ends. There are no deletions or fumblings, no lines are dropped. For example:

> The ferry pole fell
> Deep in the dark water – poked
> In the eye of god

The ferryman's son knows he could not drop the pole in mistake. Throw him in the river. To warn the rest.

> *The* FIRST SOLDIER *disappears from the window. The* SECOND SOLDIER *goes out. A moment later he's seen crossing the open window.* BASHO *goes out and disappears in the other direction – he doesn't cross the window.*
> *Sounds off.*

FIRST SOLDIER (*off*). Hey!

THIRD SOLDIER (*off*). Up!

> *Off, a splash.*

FERRYMAN (*off*). Ah – I – ah –
SECOND SOLDIER (*off*). Hold him.
THIRD SOLDIER (*off*). The pole.
FERRYMAN (*off*). Ah – ah –

Off, splashing and the sound of a wet bundle being hit. The
WIFE *rises and slowly crosses the room towards the window. As*
she moves she fumbles with her gag. She stops in exhaustion. She
does not reach the window. She is silent.

THIRD SOLDIER (*off*). Hit him.
SECOND SOLDIER (*off. Annoyed*). You do it!

Off, the sound of the wet bundle being hit. More splashing.

FERRYMAN (*off*). Uh – uh –
SECOND SOLDIER (*off*). His hands!

The WIFE *removes her gag. Immediately, as if tuned in on a*
radio, the weak, persistent sound of her cry, on one note.

THIRD SOLDIER (*off*). Kick!
FIRST SOLDIER (*off*). Why do they struggle at that age?
FERRYMAN (*off*). Uh –
SECOND SOLDIER (*off*). Cantankerous old sod.
FERRYMAN (*off*). Uh –

Off, a few splashes. The WIFE'S *cry ends.*

NINE

BASHO's *house. Night. He sits at the writing table. Paper and other*
writing materials on the table before him. He is listening intensely.
TO-SI, *his servant boy, waits in fear. In the distance, a shot.*

BASHO (*calmly*). There – again! A shot.

Another shot, off, in the distance. No other sound.

BASHO. To-si, send the chief soldier to me.

TO-SI. Sir. (*Crosses to the door.*)

BASHO. If he can be spared.

TO-SI (*stops, bows*). Sir.

> TO-SI *goes out left.* BASHO *starts to collect manuscripts. He stops in uncertainty.*

BASHO (*calls*). To-si!

> *No answer.* BASHO *hurries round the room with more manuscripts. He stacks them on the table.* KUNG-TU *hurries in left.*

KUNG-TU. Why aren't the soldiers fighting? The village is being attacked. (*Sees papers.*) What are you doing?

BASHO (*calls*). To-si! – I sent my boy for the captain. Keep calm. Official documents.

KUNG-TU. They're poems! Are you leaving? They'll burn my store!

BASHO. How many were there?

KUNG-TU. How could I tell? It's dark! There was shooting. I bumped into people. And a donkey. D'you want me to count the donkeys! Half the people here will join them!

> *The* FIRST SOLDIER *comes in.*

FIRST SOLDIER. The village is being attacked.

BASHO. What are you doing to –

FIRST SOLDIER. Nothing.

KUNG-TU. Nothing?

BASHO. But what –

KUNG-TU. They'll burn my store! Our homes! My family's in –

FIRST SOLDIER. Shut up! I know. (*To* BASHO.) My men went to look. The military beacons have been fired up the river. That means a concerted attack on all villages.

KUNG-TU. Why was it allowed to get so far? I'll complain to –

BASHO. Why aren't you doing –

FIRST SOLDIER. I'm following orders.

BASHO. Preposterous! What time have you had for orders? As judge I order you to hand over to the second in command.

KUNG-TU (*fear*). O god.

FIRST SOLDIER. I came here with orders. The decision was made two years ago. We were to try to contain the situation. If we failed or there was a serious attack: withdrawal to the provincial capital. That must be defended at all costs.

BASHO. Then the government's hollow within.

FIRST SOLDIER (*shrugs*). I must go to my men.

KUNG-TU (*sudden, short, sharp yelps of panic. Pure animal sound*). Yu! Yu! Yu! Yu! Yu!

BASHO. You abandon us!

KUNG-TU. Traitor!

> KUNG-TU *hits the* FIRST SOLDIER *awkwardly. The* FIRST SOLDIER *pushes him off, he won't waste his energy.*

FIRST SOLDIER. I'm sorry, I haven't time.

KUNG-TU. My stocks – rice, corn, oil – well, a little fortune. All cased. Ready to move. Send your soldiers. It'll be worth your while.

FIRST SOLDIER. We're not a baggage train. We must move fast or we'll –

KUNG-TU. Take me. I'm not rich, you know – but there's money in – (*hesitates*).

FIRST SOLDIER. My men will need paying too.

> TO-SI *comes back left. Bursts of distant firing are heard from time to time but nothing is seen.*

TO-SI. They're burning your shop.

KUNG-TU. You have an army outside and you haven't fired a shot!

FIRST SOLDIER (*to* KUNG-TU). I'm going.

> KUNG-TU *produces a roll of notes.*

KUNG-TU (*gestures vaguely, he has an almost sexual embarrassment over the notes*). You see . . .

FIRST SOLDIER. I'll ask the men.

KUNG-TU (*wheedling*). Just a few cases. There's Korean tea. A few rolls of – there's oil –

FIRST SOLDIER. My men get their hands on that – d'you think you'll see any of it? It'll be all I can do to stop them vanishing over the fields – without giving them loot to take!

KUNG-TU. I'll fetch my family.

FIRST SOLDIER (*to* BASHO). And you?

BASHO. My poems!

FIRST SOLDIER (*stares at* BASHO). You'll have to carry them in your head. (*Goes left towards door.*)

BASHO. Why wasn't I warned? The government sent me no instructions.

FIRST SOLDIER (*shrugs*). The landowner must have got them. I expect he forgot to pass them on when he left.

The FIRST SOLDIER *goes out left.*

BASHO. To-si, go to them. They won't hurt you. Tell them I'll receive them. Say there will be an arrangement. Pardons.

TO-SI *goes out left.*

KUNG-TU. You think they'll come?

KUNG-TU *sits uncertainly. More sporadic bursts of firing, off.*

I ought to fetch my family. The children could carry a few sacks. (*Figuratively biting his nails.*) O god it's like an examination. What is it best to do? If we run and get caught – that would be worst! Should I risk it and stay? (*Looks at* BASHO.) If they come, what will you give them?

BASHO (*fingering his poems*). What?

KUNG-TU. What will you –

BASHO (*cutting him short*). I'm not sure.

KUNG-TU. You must be sure! I'm betrayed on all sides. The

moment we're out of town the soldiers will cut my throat. I'll tell them about my – you see, there's a small account in the capital. Not much, but enough for this. If I promise – when we get there –? I wasn't born rich. I'm *not* rich! But I gave my life to my store. Now? Perhaps my wife will bring a few cases. (*Cries.*) She's a good woman. And my son's got a strong back. He could manage two.

Noises outside. KUNG-TU *runs to the door left to listen.*

KUNG-TU. Soldiers leaving. (*Panicking.*) My money!
SECOND SOLDIER (*off*). Light out.
FOURTH SOLDIER (*off*). Out!
KUNG-TU (*turns back to* BASHO). Tell my wife. She'll catch us up.

KUNG-TU *goes out left.* BASHO *starts collecting manuscripts again. He puts some on the table. They slither off.*

TEN

River bank. Mid-day. WANG, PU-TOI, SHEOUL, LU, KAKA, TOR-QUO *and others eat their bread. Shovels stacked like rifles. On one side* PU-TOI *mends a shovel. He reshapes the bottom end of the wooden handle and nails the spade back on to it.* SHEOUL *helps him and eats at the same time.*

TOR-QUO. My wife doesn't want to live by the river.
SAN-KO. When the banks are mended?
TOR-QUO. So she says.
SAN-KO. Handy for fish.
TOR-QUO. I told her.
LU (*laughs*).
TOR-QUO. What's funny in that?
LU. San-ko wiggles his feet when he talks.

SAN-KO. No I don't.
LU. You do. Say something.
SAN-KO. No.
KAKA. Coward.
SAN-KO. You're all looking.
PU-TOI (*to* SHEOUL). A bigger nail.

SHEOUL *searches in the nail can.*

WANG. Is she afraid of the river?
TOR-QUO (*shrugs*). Perhaps.
LU. A lot are.
KAKA. The banks won't break now.
SHEOUL (*to* PU-TOI). That do?
PU-TOI. Fine.
TOR-QUO. People remember the river. Young people, it's different
for them. They don't know what the past means.
PU-TOI (*hammering. To* SHEOUL). Be more careful.
SHEOUL. I was.
PU-TOI. Next time it sticks don't bend it. Lift it out cleanly and
try again.
SHEOUL. Something to eat?
PU-TOI. Please.

SHEOUL *crosses to* LU.

TOR-QUO. Are you afraid of the river?
SHEOUL. No.
LU. Would your wife move?
SHEOUL. Pu-toi hasn't eaten yet.
LU (*putting food in a bowl*). Anyone else?
TOR-QUO (*nods*). Me.
SAN-KO. Me. See – my feet didn't move.
SHEOUL (*taking a bowl from* LU). Thank you.
LU. Because you stopped them.

SAN-KO *groans in disgust.*

I don't mind them wiggling. I like it.

SAN-KO. It's odd.

LU (*to* TOR-QUO). I wouldn't move. Here's grandad for the bowls. Grandad –!

The HUSBAND, *from Scene Seven, comes on. He carries a stack of bowls. Empty rice cans are looped on his arms.*

HUSBAND. Finished?

LU. – are you afraid of the river?

HUSBAND. I'm not afraid of anything.

SHEOUL (*takes the spade from* PU-TOI *and gives him the food*). Thank you.

PU-TOI. Thanks.

SHEOUL (*looks at the spade*). I couldn't break that if I tried.

PU-TOI (*eating*). We'll see.

LU. Bowls please. (*She collects bowls for the* HUSBAND.) Aren't you afraid of the dark?

HUSBAND. No.

LU. Tigers?

HUSBAND. No.

LU. Landowners?

HUSBAND. I'm not afraid of anything, my dear. I try not to be.

LU. Not even the water when the banks are broken?

SAN-KO. Why should the banks break? We'll build them well. It's for our own sake. There'll be locks. A cut-off channel for the spring tides. The banks will have stone walls. We're changing the river. What's the matter with you? You speak as if the old river was there. We have a –

The others roar with laughter.

Now what?

WANG. Your feet!

LU. They're wagging!

SAN-KO. They're not!

KAKA. They are! They are!

SAN-KO. Of course they are! I'm telling the truth! Your feet ought to waggle when you tell the truth! They're still when you lie! Or you're dead!

LU (*puts an arm round* SAN-KO's *neck*). San-ko I'm joking!

SAN-KO. It's good when my feet waggle! Look!

The others laugh.

HUSBAND. I don't understand you young people half the time. (*Calls loudly.*) Work in five minutes. (*Crosses to* PU-TOI.) Not finished? What's wrong with your appetite? When I was your age –

VOICE (*off, right*). Help!

Immediately GOW *runs across the stage from right to left, shouting as he goes.*

GOW. Quick. Quick. Tuan's in the water.

The others jump up and run out left after GOW. SHEOUL *is left on the stage holding her shovel. The* HUSBAND *stands a little way behind her.*

WANG (*off, running*). How long's he been in?

GOW (*off, running*). Who saw?

WANG (*off, running*). Why didn't he call?

VOICE (*off, still*). Hit his head on the bottom.

Incoherent distant sound. SHEOUL *and the* HUSBAND *stare off.*

GOW (*off, still*). His leg.

Silence. SHEOUL *puts her spade on the ground. The* HUSBAND *doesn't move. The crowd comes back with* TUAN's *body.* TOR-QUO *points to a place on the ground. They lay the body there. They stand in silence.*

TOR-QUO. Dead hours.

WANG. We need a stretcher.

They go. SHEOUL *and* LU *are the last. They stare at the body.*
LU *cries against* SHEOUL. SHEOUL *comforts her as they follow
the others out, left. In the silence* BASHO *comes from the right.
He is old and weak. He clutches a few charred manuscripts. His
clothes and skin are smudged with soot.*

BASHO. Where is the . . . ? . . . I sat in my court . . . After it was
burned . . . I woke. A rat sat in a cobweb on a dead man's head
and watched me . . . (*Goes to the corpse.*) Show me the way to
the deep north . . . I am old . . . respect my age . . . my robe of
office . . . where is enlightenment? . . . where can I find it before
I die? . . . (*Touches the corpse.*) Your face is stern . . . You have
found the way . . . Master, tell me . . . Don't turn away . . .
(*Shakes the corpse violently.*) Tell me . . . The way . . . The way
. . . (*Clambers across the corpse and shakes it.*) I will be told! Tell
me the way! . . . Or I will shake the life from your soul . . .
(*Hits at corpse.*) The way! . . .

   The others have come back. They stare. They carry a stretcher.

WANG. Basho . . . the man is dead.
BASHO. What? . . . Who is it? . . . When they burned my court the
light was so bright . . . Since then I see . . . only a few . . . the
skin has fallen over my eyes . . . soft and cold as a bat . . . My
eyes are old . . . Where is the narrow road to the deep north? . . .
Tell me . . . Please . . . I am a lost child . . . Who will show me
the way?

   BASHO *gropes down to the audience. He is bent, black and as old
   as time. His hands as he walks are near the ground. His stick
   reaches high over his back.*

SHEOUL. To do that to a corpse!
LU. It doesn't matter when the living disturb the dead.
WANG. Yes, remember: there is a worse story. Once a man lived
by a river. (*The rest nod silently in agreement. They already know
the story. They go to* TUAN, *lay him gently on the stretcher, and*

prepare to carry him out. WANG *talks as if the story were the funeral oration.*) A king came. He said to the man carry me over the river on your back. The man obeyed –

BASHO (*crying in the audience*). Where is the narrow road to the deep north?

WANG. When he reached the shore the king spoke again. Carry me over the plain to my house. The man carried him for a year. Then he asked the king when they would reach his house. The king said I'll tell you when we are there but I cannot speak till then – I have many things to think of. So the man carried him –

> *The bearers lift* TUAN *on the stretcher and begin to carry him out – not on their shoulders but at the height a medical stretcher is carried. The other people follow them.*

BASHO (*in the audience angrily banging his staff on the ground*). The narrow road to the deep north!

WANG. – for many years and the king did not speak. Each night he laid him on the ground. Each morning he took him on his back. The man did not know that the king had died long ago. So he carried him always and wasted his life. That is the worse story. To carry the dead on your back.

BASHO (*in the audience. Old and as feeble as a child. Cries*). Where is the way . . . the way . . . the way . . . ?

> BASHO *goes. The bearers and the others have already taken* TUAN *away.* WANG *is alone on the stage. As he speaks the lights begin to come up.*

WANG. We live in a time of great change. It is easy to find monsters – and as easy to find heroes. To judge rightly what is good – to choose between good and evil – that is all that it is to be human.

The Bundle Poems

THE TREE

The tree has stood before my house for eighty years
In good years the branches heavy with blossom and leaves
In bad years surviving
The branches bare only in winter
When the tree and the earth sleep

In that time the rule in the local school hasn't changed
The old gods are still worshipped
Most of the dead are buried in their name
Wages and prices have risen
There is no order
On the heath a missile site where the gibbet stood
And the young have been cut down twice

The tree endures the changing seasons
We cannot wait for spring or live long in winter
We cannot
We must change

WHO CAN CHOOSE?

Each man walks out his life in his small circle
Lifted from his cradle by elders
Borne to his grave by sons
And in that small circle
Works and laughs
Argues for or against reason
Loves and mourns
And is made weaker or stronger by neighbours

He is born in his spring and dies in his winter
But his seasons are ruled by other men's lives
Who can choose?

Great storms rock his chair
Or he opens his door to the fury
Avalanches gently push him one step
Or he leaps over cracks as they open in mountains
Seas wash his hands or he swims through them
Armies whisper into his ear
Or he asks who leads them and why they fight
He sleeps in his quiet world
Or goes out to the cry in the street
He waits till the storm batters his house
And crowds stand at his door
Or he asks: what is justice?

He can choose

VERDICT

How shall we judge this man?
By the best he did or the worst?
If we judge by the best
All men are saints

He gave to the poor
Sheltered the homeless
Visited the sick
Fed the neglected
Throw him into the fire!

What did he do to change the world?
How many suffer because he did nothing to change it?
Yet he pitied the suffering because the world wasn't changed!
Into the fire!

CRIMES

The unjust temper injustice with pity
The merciless give mercy
Just as tradesmen to make a profit
Mark some goods down

Those who teach ignorance
Endow libraries
And found great colleges
To teach it in

Barbarians patronize art
Would you expect the rich
To keep ugly whores?

Many shout peace!
Before their armies banners flutter
As if an invisible hand
Was struggling to rip them off
And throw them away

Perhaps this is their greatest crime –
Not the centuries of exploitation and violence
But their occasional use of virtue?

LOVE AND PITY

Men are formed by their rulers
Or in the struggle against them
Our minds are created by fear and obedience
Or by that struggle

What is pity?
To break the yoke on the ox's neck?
The yoke-maker has a hundred yokes in his store
Break the yoke-maker!

You break the glass in the prison window
You have not broken the iron bars
In the prison window
That is harder!
Pity is pitiless to those who serve her!

What is love?
To cry for the hungry and lost?
They can cry for themselves

Let the powerful love and pity mankind
Let the powerless love each other
No one else!

When the calf is seen to weep for the butcher
The time for change has come!

SACRIFICE

You tie the calf to the post
The ropes aren't too tight
You polish the hooves
Nuzzle the crown
Stick flowers behind its ears
Sweep up the dung it drops in fright
Mop the tears from its jowls
With your hanky
Its lips pull back at your touch
You grin at the big teeth
Even your last curse
Begins with its pet name

As it jerks in the ropes
You make your mark in its neck –
    The gash

FIRST WORLD WAR POETS

You went to the front like sheep
And bleated at the pity of it
In academies that smell of abattoirs
Your poems are still studied

You turned the earth to mud
Yet complain you drowned in it
Your generals were dug in at the rear
Degenerates drunk on brandy and prayer
You *saw* the front – and only bleated
The pity!

You survived
Did you burn your generals' houses?
Loot the new millionaires?
No, you found new excuses
You'd lost an arm or your legs
You sat by the empty fire
And hummed music hall songs

Why did your generals send you away to die?
They were afraid of the Great War that was coming
Between masters and workers
In their own land
So they herded you over the cliffs to be rid of you
How they hated you while you lived!
How they wept over you once you were dead!

What did you fight for?
A new world?
No – an old world already in ruins!
Your children?
Millions of children died
Because you fought for your enemies
And not against them!

We will not forget!
We will not forgive!

THE SAMARITAN

A merchant travelling
On business to Sidon
Saw at the roadside
A naked man
Filthy bruised bound
(Words taken at random
From the history books)

He crossed the road
He saw under the trees
Three soldiers

Who said
We're taking him to be crucified
By the port gate of Sidon

The merchant asked what he had done

They said
For six years he robbed merchants on this road
Throwing their naked bodies in ditches

The merchant said I will give him water

Three hands shot out like lizards' tongues
The merchant dropped one silver coin
On each palm
The fingers shut – bars of a trap

The merchant poured water into his bowl
He held it out to the thief
The thief did not open his mouth

A soldier kicked his ribs
A soldier prised open his jaws with his fists
A soldier emptied the bowl into his throat

The merchant took the bowl
Wiped it
And left

POEM

They run the clinic in which you're born
Christen you in their church
Teach you the rules of their school
Examine your minds
Mark them
Donate your playing field
Teach you the rules of their games
Employ you and pay you
Pay you when there's no work
Print your money
Marry you in their church or their registry office
Christen your children
Censor your television
Let you listen to their radio
Share their newspapers with you
Sweep your street
Train your police
Give you medals
Encourage you with bonuses
Punish you when you're a nuisance
Put you in hospital when you're sick
Take you into care when you're old
Burn you in their crematorium
Scatter your ash in their garden

No wonder some of you fight for them
When the rest start to ask
Who the hell they are!

DE QUÉ SIRVE UNA TAZE?

You knock out the teeth
Twist the neck till the skin is taut
As wrinkles on ice
Scorch the hair as you do on a pig
Tie the hands
And break them with a hammer
Dress the body in rags
As if it were a wound
Empty the skull
And stuff it with sheets
Torn from your book
Shoot out the eyes
So the face looks like cracked glass
And now you offer a cup

What use is a cup?

THE WATER SELLER AND THE SOLDIER

On the street the water seller
Meets a soldier and his prisoner
The prisoner asks for water
But has no money to buy it

Though the soldier forbids the water seller
To give the prisoner water
The water seller could bribe the soldier
But he is poor and must sell his water

And though the soldier
Would arrest the water seller
If he smiled to comfort the prisoner
As it is forbidden to fraternize with prisoners
(Unless the water seller had bribed the soldier
To permit him to smile at the prisoner –
An event so unlikely it can be discounted
Even by poets)
It so happens that the water seller
Does not choose to smile at the prisoner
(Or anyone else for that matter)
Because lately many water sellers' water
Was stolen on this very street

Thus the soldier defends the water seller
So that his trade may prosper
And his life be happy and good
But the water seller can't do this good deed
Nor even smile
(Had he chosen to smile)
Because the soldier defends him

So the water seller and the soldier
Smile at each other

Is this the behaviour of rational beings?

VIRTUE

We wish to be kind
To speak gently
To comfort the sufferers
We would walk over continents to feed the hungry
Build shelters for those made homeless by storms
Sit with the aged and talk to the bewildered

It is not time to sit and talk
We have not earned the right to be kind
We have not won the power to do good
In our world only the evil are clothed in virtue
And a good deed arouses suspicion

Then be hard!
Be unforgiving!
Do not be patient!
How else shall we find justice?

CULTURE

What is culture?
The best? – Too vague!

Who owns the tool?
The man with money
Who uses the tool?
The tool user
What does the tool do?
Change the relationship
Between men and the world
Who owns the tool user?
The man with money
What does the tool do?
Change society
What is society?
The relationship between
Owner and user

What is culture?
Taking power from the owner
To give to the user
That is culture
The highest the human mind
Can aspire to!
The passing of power
From owner to user
Creates virtue and art
Nothing else raises
Men over the beast
Whatever hinders this passing of power
Is against culture
Culture is this change

WHAT IS WANTED

I wanted to smile
But I saw how the evil smiled
I wanted to share
But I learned that long after I'd given
All I had
The poor would be poor
I did not want anger
I'd heard of the saint who found freedom in prison
But this only comforts gaolers
Above all I wanted peace
For I knew war

But what I wanted is not yet to be had
Now I want something else:
That one day it will be

For that I would give up
All I had wanted

ESSAY ON THE SELLERS OF WATER

1.

Water sellers sell water to the poor
The groans of the poor are pitiful
Why don't the water sellers give water
At least to the poorest?

In the merchant world everything is priced
A green paper fluttering in the storm
Is scrap or a banknote –
Which is decided by the world of the merchant
Though both flutter like a leaf in the storm

Men too flutter in the storm
And whether they're scrap or worth money
The world of the merchant decides

2.

Every commodity has a price
The price tags are clear to be seen on the counter
But in the world of the merchant all things are priced
Acts thoughts dreams regrets – all priced
Just as all things on earth cast a shadow

It is a law:
When one thing is priced all things are priced
The water seller prays for drought
To keep up the price of water
And so he prays that the world of the merchant stands firm
And therefore that all things shall keep their price

See! the water in the bowl
Creates the water seller
He earns his life by selling water
His life is shaped by the laws of selling
His world lives by the laws of selling
His morals are based on the laws of selling
All his laws are laws of selling!

If the water seller can't give his water
At least he can smile at the poor?
No! – when one thing is priced all things are priced
To give water ruins the price of water
To smile freely destroys the value of virtue
It replaces the law of selling with a new law
But in the world of the merchant
Virtue depends on the price of water
So to smile you must first change the world
The man who smiles does not wish to sell water
The water seller can only simper or grin

3.

The merchant thinks that at evening
He shuts his shutters and goes – leaving the market
No! – the whole of his life is bought and sold
His world is a tree that roots in the market
The topmost leaf and the smallest twig
Grow from its gutter

The merchant is like a boy in an apple tree
When the wind blows his body contorts
His arms stiffen like branches
The apples hang from his hands
The wind blows through him
And he has become part of the tree

He may reach for the highest apple
But the wind still blows or the bough bends
And shapes the boy to the tree

The merchant believes he has hours of peace
~~~ ~~~~~~~~ ~~ ~~~~~~~ are checked

ERATTUM

p. 98, line 6 should read:

No! – even time flows like water from the municipal conduit

Even silence and stillness
Religion virtue culture and love
All buying and selling
Bubbling and seething

4.

And one day the spring water rises
And sweeps the merchants and soldiers out to the ocean
Like rubbish thrown behind a mountain

There is also this law:
When one thing is not priced nothing is priced
The water carried to the streets is not changed
But the laws are changed
The powers that force the laws are changed
The men that carry the water are changed

The spring water rises and merchants and soldiers are swept away
Like trash thrown over a mountain
And the value of water is judged
Not by what it earns
But the thirst it quenches
And all things are changed

Methuen's Modern Plays

Methuen's New Theatrescripts

Theatrescripts aim to close the gap between the appearance of new work in the theatre and its publication in script form. The emphasis is on new or unconventional work, and the price is kept as low as possible.

Methuen's Theatre Classics

The Master Playwrights

Collections of plays by the best-known modern playwrights in value-for-money paperbacks.

Edward Bond

PLAYS: ONE
The Pope's Wedding, Saved, Early Morning

Joe Orton

THE COMPLETE PLAYS
The Ruffian on the Stair, Entertaining Mr Sloane, Loot, The Erpingham Camp, The Good and Faithful Servant, Funeral Games, What the Butler Saw

Harold Pinter

PLAYS: ONE
The Room, The Dumb Waiter, the Birthday Party, A Slight Ache, A Night Out

PLAYS: TWO
The Caretaker, Night School, The Dwarfs, The Collection, The Lover, five revue sketches

Strindberg

THE FATHER, MISS JULIE, THE GHOST SONATA
Translated with introductions by Michael Meyer

If you would like regular information on new Methuen plays and theatre books, please write to:

The Marketing Department
Eyre Methuen Ltd
North Way
Andover
Hants

DATE DUE	
MAR 2 0 1993	